MOLECULAR PATHOLOGY AND
THE DYNAMICS OF DISEASE

MOLECULAR PATHOLOGY AND THE DYNAMICS OF DISEASE

MAIKA G. MITCHELL

ACADEMIC PRESS

An imprint of Elsevier

Academic Press is an imprint of Elsevier
125 London Wall, London EC2Y 5AS, United Kingdom
525 B Street, Suite 1800, San Diego, CA 92101-4495, United States
50 Hampshire Street, 5th Floor, Cambridge, MA 02139, United States
The Boulevard, Langford Lane, Kidlington, Oxford OX5 1GB, United Kingdom

British Library Cataloguing-in-Publication Data
A catalogue record for this book is available from the British Library

Library of Congress Cataloging-in-Publication Data
A catalog record for this book is available from the Library of Congress

ISBN: 978-0-12-814610-1

For Information on all Academic Press publications
visit our website at https://www.elsevier.com/books-and-journals

Working together
to grow libraries in
developing countries

www.elsevier.com • www.bookaid.org

Publisher: John Fedor
Acquisition Editor: Tari K. Broderick
Editorial Project Manager: Timothy Bennett
Production Project Manager: Punithavathy Govindaradjane
Cover Designer: Matthew Limbert

Typeset by MPS Limited, Chennai, India

Dedication

Nothing in life happens without support. My loving family—my husband and my beautiful children. They have endured my late night writing and early morning discussions of the topics within this book.

The goal has been achieved of leaving a legacy and body of work for my children and future generations to be proud of from this moment forward.

Enjoy!

Contents

Preface   ix

1. Molecular Pathology Introduction and Research Review   1

Pathogenesis Overview and Review   1
Incubation Period   11
Multiplication in Target Organs   12
Shedding of Virus   13
Congenital Infections   14
NK Cells in Hepatitis C Virus Infection   14
Conclusions   15
References   16
Further Reading   17

2. Challenges in Molecular Pathology   19

General Overview of Molecular Applications in Pathology   22
Technical Obstacles for the Molecular Diagnostic Industry
     and in the Pathology Laboratory   23
Technological Challenges in Molecular Assays   23
Mutation Detection in Precision Medicine   24
Detection of Chromosomal Rearrangements: In Situ Hybridization   25
Validation of Comprehensive Molecular Assays   26
Quality Management Program   26
References   53
Further Reading   54

3. Review of Clinical Human Medical Genetics   55

Deoxyribonucleic Acid (DNA)   55
Context of Clinical Human Genetics   60
References   73
Further Reading   74

4. Molecular Medicine in Action 77

Grossing Procedures 77
Specimen Adequacy 89
Specimen Collection Instructions 92
Immunohistochemistry and HPV In Situ Procedures 106
Kwik-Diff Staining 128
Non-GYN Staining 132
Gram Stain Method: Hucker's Modification 135
Gomori's Trichrome Stain 140
Acid-Fast Bacilli Stain for Mycobacteria 144
Destaining Procedure 147

5. Mechanisms of Disease 151

NK Cells in CMV Infection 157
NK Cells in HIV-1 Infection 157
References 158
Further Reading 159

Index 169

Preface

Molecular Pathology and the Dynamics of Disease, the first edition, is the improved understanding of the cellular and molecular mechanisms of diseases. Novel molecular assays not only aid in a disease diagnosis, but also disease prognosis. Similarly modulation of biological pathways for the treatment of a disease is becoming a reality. The molecular structure and function of a normal and abnormal gene product enables the determination of highly relevant diagnostic, therapeutic, and prognostic information.

Classically trained physicians and scientists, respectively, are bombarded daily with basic standard-of-care and translational data on the mechanisms of health and disease. It is of great significance to generate technological resources capable of:

1. bridging chemistry and pathology, and molecular medicine;
2. providing a unique educational resource to the physician-scientist and researchers keeping abreast of the timely advances, evolving modalities, and shifting paradigms; and
3. providing fundamental SOPs detailing concepts in molecular medicine. *Molecular Pathology and the Dynamics of Disease* is a compilation of a broad range of topics in pathogenesis that serves as a unique, timely, and comprehensive resource for practicing physicians, researchers, and data scientists (bioinformaticians) in the ever-evolving field of integrative and personalized medicine.

Molecular Pathology and the Dynamics of Disease integrates the traditional knowledge of physiological and pathological processes with a balanced emphasis on fundamental concepts, timely advances in cellular and molecular mechanisms, and applied pathology. The textbook is organized into several sections, each of which includes chapters that progressively and cohesively elaborate on pertinent SOPs in molecular medicine and molecular pathology.

The textbook is written and presented as a one-stop and comprehensive reference on molecular medicine for basic, translational and clinical researchers, bioinformaticians, and physicians. I anticipate this textbook to be of value to pathologists, oncologists, molecular biologists, physiologists, biochemists, and immunohistochemists. This textbook is also suitable for medical students, graduate students, residents, clinical laboratorians, and fellows with an interest in molecular biology. The format of the textbook is meant to serve as a ready reference to relevant topics in the molecular-based medicine, thus providing a practical disease-based integrative resource on the molecular pathology of disease.

Maika G. Mitchell

1

Molecular Pathology Introduction and Research Review

Molecular pathology, a rapidly expanding discipline connecting pathology and molecular biology, is providing a deeper insight and understanding of the molecular basis of the etiology and pathogenesis of human disease. This well-laid-out book covers the basic principles of molecular pathology, explains the most important molecular diagnostic techniques in user-friendly language, and describes their applications across a broad range of human diseases and problems, including cancer, hereditary disorders, identity testing, and infectious diseases.

PATHOGENESIS OVERVIEW AND REVIEW

Pathogenesis is the process by which an infection leads to disease. Pathogenic mechanisms of viral disease include (1) implantation of virus at the portal of entry, (2) local replication, (3) spread to target organs (disease sites), and (4) spread to sites of shedding of virus into the environment. Factors that affect pathogenic mechanisms are (1) accessibility of virus to tissue, (2) cell susceptibility to virus multiplication, and (3) virus susceptibility to host defenses. Natural selection favors the dominance of low-virulence virus strains.

Direct cell damage and death from viral infection may result from (1) diversion of the cell's energy, (2) shutoff of cell macromolecular synthesis, (3) competition of viral mRNA for cellular ribosomes, and (4) competition of viral promoters and transcriptional enhancers for cellular transcriptional factors such as RNA polymerases, and inhibition of the interferon (IFN) defense mechanisms. Indirect cell damage can

1

result from integration of the viral genome, induction of mutations in the host genome, inflammation, and the host immune response.

Viral affinity for specific body tissues (tropism) is determined by (1) cell receptors for virus, (2) cell transcription factors that recognize viral promoters and enhancer sequences, (3) ability of the cell to support virus replication, (4) physical barriers, (5) local temperature, pH, and oxygen tension enzymes and nonspecific factors in body secretions, and (6) digestive enzymes and bile in the gastrointestinal tract that may inactivate some viruses.

Virions implant onto living cells mainly via the respiratory, gastrointestinal, skin-penetrating, and genital routes although other routes can be used. The final outcome of infection may be determined by the dose and location of the virus as well as its infectivity and virulence.

Most virus types spread among cells extracellularly, but some may also spread intracellularly. Establishment of local infection may lead to localized disease and localized shedding of virus.

Viremic: The most common route of systemic spread from the portal of entry is the circulation, which the virus reaches via the lymphatics. Virus may enter the target organs from the capillaries by (1) multiplying in endothelial cells or fixed macrophages, (2) diffusing through gaps, and (3) being carried in a migrating leukocyte.

Neural: Dissemination via nerves usually occurs with rabies virus and sometimes with herpesvirus and poliovirus infections.

The incubation period is the time between exposure to virus and onset of disease. During this usually asymptomatic period, implantation, local multiplication, and spread (for disseminated infections) occur.

Depending on the balance between virus and host defenses, virus multiplication in the target organ may be sufficient to cause disease and death.

Although the respiratory tract, alimentary tract, urogenital tract, and blood are the most frequent sites of shedding, diverse viruses may be shed at virtually every site.

Infection of the fetus as a target "organ" is special because the virus must traverse additional physical barriers, the early fetal immune and interferon defense systems may be immature, transfer of the maternal defenses are partially blocked by the placenta, the developing first-trimester fetal organs are vulnerable to infection, and hormonal changes are taking place.

Pathogenesis is the process by which virus infection leads to disease. Pathogenic mechanisms include implantation of the virus at a body site (the portal of entry), replication at that site, and then spread to and multiplication within sites (target organs) where disease or shedding of virus into the environment occurs. Most viral infections are subclinical, suggesting that body defenses against viruses arrest most infections before disease symptoms become manifest. Knowledge of subclinical infections comes from serologic studies showing that sizeable portions of the population have specific antibodies to viruses even though the individuals have no history of disease. These inapparent infections have great epidemiologic importance: they constitute major sources for dissemination of virus through the population, and they confer immunity.

Many factors affect pathogenic mechanisms. An early determinant is the extent to which body tissues and organs are accessible to the virus. Accessibility is influenced by physical barriers (such as mucus and tissue barriers), by the distance to be traversed within the body, and by natural defense mechanisms. If the virus reaches an organ, infection occurs only if cells capable of supporting virus replication are present. Cellular susceptibility requires a cell surface attachment site (receptor) for the virions and also an intracellular environment that permits virus replication and release. Even if virus initiates infection in a susceptible organ, replication of sufficient virus to cause disease may be prevented by host defenses.

Other factors that determine whether infection and disease occur are the many virulence characteristics of the infecting virus. To cause disease, the infecting virus must be able to overcome the inhibitory effects of physical barriers, distance, host defenses, and differing cellular susceptibilities to infection. The inhibitory effects are genetically controlled and therefore may vary among individuals and races. Virulence characteristics enable the virus to initiate infection, spread in the body, and replicate to large enough numbers to impair the target organ. These factors include the ability to replicate under certain circumstances during inflammation, during the febrile response, in migratory cells, and in the presence of natural body inhibitors and interferon. Extremely virulent strains often occur within virus populations. Occasionally, these strains become dominant as a result of unusual selective pressures. The viral proteins and genes responsible for specific virulence functions are only just beginning to be identified.

Fortunately for the survival of humans and animals, most natural selective pressures favor the dominance of less virulent strains. Because these strains do not cause severe disease or death, their replication and transmission are not impaired by an incapacitated host. Mild or inapparent infections can result from absence of one or more virulence factors. For example, a virus that has all the virulence characteristics except the ability to multiply at elevated temperatures is arrested at the febrile stage of infection and causes a milder disease than its totally virulent counterpart. Live virus vaccines are composed of viruses deficient in one or more virulence factors; they cause only inapparent infections and yet are able to replicate sufficiently to induce immunity.

The occurrence of spontaneous or induced mutations in viral genetic material may alter the pathogenesis of the induced disease, e.g., HIV. These mutations can be of particular importance with the development of drug resistant strains of virus.

Disease does not always follow successful virus replication in the target organ. Disease occurs only if the virus replicates sufficiently to damage essential cells directly, to cause the release of toxic substances from infected tissues, to damage cellular genes or to damage organ function indirectly as a result of the host immune response to the presence of virus antigens.

As a group, viruses use all conceivable portals of entry, mechanisms of spread, target organs, and sites of excretion. This abundance of possibilities is not surprising considering the astronomic numbers of viruses and their variants.

Cellular Pathogenesis

Direct cell damage and death may result from disruption of cellular macromolecular synthesis by the infecting virus. Also, viruses cannot synthesize their genetic and structural components, and so they rely almost exclusively on the host cell for these functions. Their parasitic replication therefore robs the host cell of energy and macromolecular components, severely impairing the host's ability to function and often resulting in cell death and disease.

Pathogenesis at the cellular level can be viewed as a process that occurs in progressive stages leading to cellular disease. As noted above, an essential aspect of viral pathogenesis at the cellular level is the competition between the synthetic needs of the virus and those of the host cell. Since viruses must use the cell's machinery to synthesize their own nucleic acids and proteins, they have evolved various mechanisms to subvert the cell's normal functions to those required for production of viral macromolecules and eventually viral progeny. The function of some of the viral genetic elements associated with virulence may be related to providing conditions in which the synthetic needs of the virus compete effectively for a limited supply of cellular macromolecule components and synthetic machinery, such as ribosomes.

Most viruses have an affinity for specific tissues; that is, they display tissue specificity or tropism. This specificity is determined by selective susceptibility of cells, physical barriers, local temperature and pH, and host defenses. Many examples of viral tissue tropism are known. Polioviruses selectively infect and destroy certain nerve cells, which have a higher concentration of surface receptors for polioviruses than do virus-resistant cells. Rhinoviruses multiply exclusively in the upper respiratory tract because they are adapted to multiply best at low temperature and pH and high oxygen tension. Enteroviruses can multiply in the intestine, partly because they resist inactivation by digestive enzymes, bile, and acid. The cell receptors for some viruses have been identified. Rabies virus uses the acetylcholine receptor present on neurons as a receptor, and hepatitis B virus binds to polymerized albumin receptors found on liver cells. Similarly, Epstein-Barr virus uses complement CD21 receptors on B lymphocytes, and human immunodeficiency virus uses the CD4 molecules present on T lymphocytes as specific receptors.

Viral tropism is also dictated in part by the presence of specific cell transcription factors that require enhancer sequences within the viral genome. Recently, enhancer sequences have been shown to participate in the pathogenesis of certain viral infections. Enhancer sequences within the long terminal repeat regions of Moloney murine leukemia retrovirus are active in certain host tissues. In addition, JV papovavirus appears to have an enhancer sequence that is active specifically in oligodendroglia cells, and hepatitis B virus enhancer activity is most active in hepatocytes.

Viruses are carried to the body by all possible routes (air, food, bites, and any contaminated object). Similarly, all possible sites of implantation (all body surfaces and internal sites reached by mechanical penetration) may be used. The frequency of implantation is greatest where virus contacts living cells directly (in the respiratory tract, in the alimentary tract, in the genital tract, and subcutaneously). With some viruses, implantation in the fetus may occur at the time of fertilization through infected germ cells, as well as later in gestation via the placenta, or at birth.

Even at the earliest stage of pathogenesis (implantation), certain variables may influence the final outcome of the infection. For example, the dose, infectivity, and virulence of virus implanted and the location of implantation may determine whether the infection will be inapparent (subclinical) or will cause mild, severe, or lethal disease.

Local Replication and Local Spread

Successful implantation may be followed by local replication and local spread of virus (Fig. 1.1). Virus that replicates within the initially infected cell may spread to adjacent cells extracellularly or intracellularly. Extracellular spread occurs by release of virus into the extracellular fluid and subsequent infection of the adjacent cell. Intracellular spread occurs by fusion of infected cells with adjacent, uninfected cells or by way of cytoplasmic bridges between cells. Most viruses spread

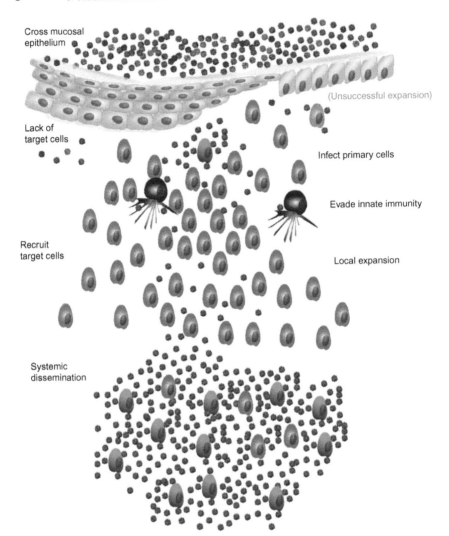

Cross mucosal epithelium

(Unsuccessful expansion)

Lack of target cells

Infect primary cells

Evade innate immunity

Recruit target cells

Local expansion

Systemic dissemination

FIGURE 1.1 Virus spread during localized infection.

extracellularly, but herpesviruses, paramyxoviruses, and poxviruses may spread through both intracellular and extracellular routes. Intracellular spread provides virus with a partially protected environment because the antibody defense does not penetrate cell membranes.

Spread to cells beyond adjacent cells may occur through the liquid spaces within the local site (e.g., lymphatics) or by diffusion through surface fluids such as the mucous layer of the respiratory tract. Also, infected migratory cells such as lymphocytes and macrophages may spread the virus within local tissue.

TABLE 1.1   Pathogenesis of Selected Virus Infection: Localized Infections

Disease	Site of Implantation	Route of Spread	Target Organ	Site of Shedding
Influenza	Respiratory tract	Local	Respiratory tract	Respiratory tract
Coryza	Respiratory tract	Local	Respiratory tract	Respiratory tract
Gastroenteritis	Alimentary tract	Local	Alimentary tract	Alimentary tract
Warts	Skin and mucosa	Local	Skin and mucosa	Skin and mucosa

Establishment of infection at the portal of entry may be followed by continued local virus multiplication, leading to localized virus shedding and localized disease. In this way, local sites of implantation also are target organs and sites of shedding in many infections (Table 1.1). Respiratory tract infections that fall into this category include influenza, the common cold, and parainfluenza virus infections. Alimentary tract infections caused by several gastroenteritis viruses (e.g., rotaviruses and picornaviruses) also may fall into this category. Localized skin infections of this type include warts, cowpox, and molluscum contagiosum. Localized infections may spread over body surfaces to infect distant surfaces. An example of this is the picornavirus epidemic conjunctivitis shown in Figs. 1.2A and B; in the absence of viremia, virus spreads directly from the eye (site of implantation) to the pharynx and intestine. Other viruses may spread internally to distant target organs and sites of excretion (disseminated infection). A third category of viruses may cause both local and disseminated disease, as in herpes simplex and measles.

Dissemination in the Bloodstream

At the portal of entry, multiplying virus contacts pathways to the blood and peripheral nerves, the principal routes of widespread dissemination through the body. The most common route of systemic spread of virus involves the circulation (Fig. 1.3 and Table 1.2). Viruses such as those causing poliomyelitis, smallpox, and measles disseminate through the blood after an initial period of replication at the portal of entry (the alimentary and respiratory tracts), where the infection often causes no significant symptoms or signs of illness because the virus kills cells that are expendable and easily replaced. Virus progeny diffuse through the afferent lymphatics to the lymphoid tissue and then through the efferent lymphatics to infect cells in close contact with the bloodstream (e.g., endothelial cells, especially those of the lymphoreticular organs). This initial spread may result in a brief primary viremia. Subsequent release

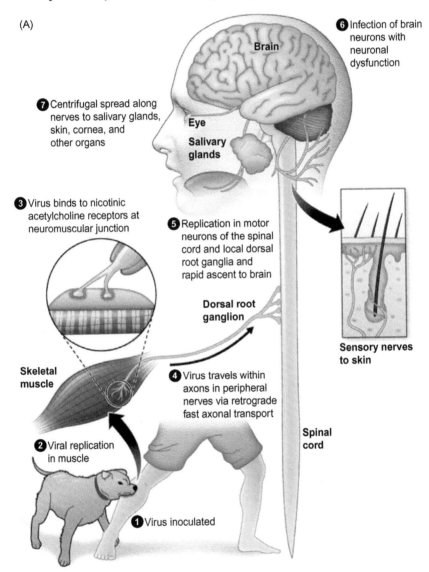

FIGURE 1.2   (A) Infections due to RNA viruses. Source: *Kasper DL, Fauci AS, Hauser SL, Longo DL, Jameson JL, Loscalzo J. Harrison's principles of internal medicine. 19th ed. AccessMedicine: McGraw-Hill Medical; 2014.* (B) Pathogenesis of infection through the body systems and the psychological effects.

(B)

Pathogenesis

- Infection of mucosal cells results in cellular destruction and desquamation of the superficial mucosa.
- The resulting edema and mononuclear cell infiltration are accompanied by local symptoms: nonproductive cough, sore throat, and nasal discharge.
- Systemic symptoms: fever, muscle aches, headache, and general prostration.

Systemic
- Fever

Psychological
- Lethargy
- Lack of appetite

Nasopharynx
- Runny nose
- Sore throat

Respiratory
- Coughing

Intestinal
- Diarrhea

Gastric
- Nausea
- Vomiting

FIGURE 1.2 (*Continued*).

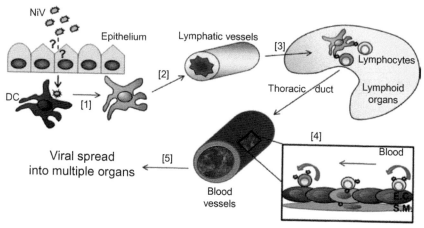

FIGURE 1.3 Virus spread through bloodstream during a generalized infection. Numbers indicate sequence of events.

of virus directly into the bloodstream induces a secondary viremia, which usually lasts several days and puts the virus in contact with the capillary system of all body tissues. Virus may enter the target organ from the capillaries by replicating within a capillary endothelial cell or fixed macrophage and then being released on the target organ side of the capillary. Virus may also diffuse through small gaps in the capillary endothelium or penetrate the capillary wall through an infected, migrating leukocyte. The virus may then replicate and spread within the target organ or site of excretion by the same mechanisms as for local dissemination at the

TABLE 1.2   Pathogenesis of Selected Virus Infections: Disseminated Infections

Disease	Common Site of Implantation	Route of Spread	Target Organ(s)	Site of Shedding
Poliomyelitis	Alimentary tract	Blood (nerves)	Central nervous system	Alimentary tract
Hepatitis A	Alimentary tract	Blood	Liver	Alimentary tract
AIDS	Injection, kauma, intestine	Blood	Immune system, brain	Blood, semen
Kuru	Alimentary tract	Blood	Brain	Brain (transmitted by ingestion)
Rubella	Respiratory tract	Blood	Skin, lymph nodes, fetus	Respiratory tract, excreta in newborn
Measles	Respiratory tract	Blood	Skin, lungs, brain	Respiratory tract
Chickenpox	Respiratory tract	Blood, nerves (to site of latency)	Skin, lungs	Respiratory tract skin

HERPES SIMPLEX TYPE 1

Acute	Respiratory tract	Nerves, leukocytes	Many (e.g., brain, liver, skin)	Respiratory tract, epithelial surfaces
Recurrent	Ganglion	Nerves (to site of latency)	Skin, eye	Skin, eyes
Rabies	Subcutaneously (bite)	Nerves	Brain	Salivary glands
Arbovirus infection	Subcutaneously (bite)	Blood	Brain and others	Lymph and blood (via insect bite)
Hepatitis B	Penetration of skin	Blood	Liver	Blood
Herpes simplex type 2	Genital tract	Nerves (to site of latency)	Genital tract	Genital tract

portal of entry. Disease occurs if the virus replicates in a sufficient number of essential cells and destroys them. For example, in poliomyelitis the central nervous system is the target organ, whereas the alimentary tract is both the portal of entry and the site of shedding. In some situations, the target organ and site of shedding may be the same.

Dissemination in Nerves

Dissemination through the nerves is less common than bloodstream dissemination, but is the means of spread in a number of important diseases (Fig. 1.4). This mechanism occurs in rabies virus, herpesvirus, and, occasionally, poliomyelitis virus infections. For example, rabies virus implanted by a bite from a rabid animal replicates subcutaneously and within muscular tissue to reach nerve endings. Evidence indicates that the virus spreads centrally in the neurites (axons and dendrites) and perineural cells, where virus is shielded from antibody. This nerve route leads rabies virus to the central nervous system, where disease originates. Rabies virus then spreads centrifugally through the nerves to reach the salivary glands, the site of shedding. Table 1.2 shows other examples of nerve spread.

INCUBATION PERIOD

During most virus infections, no signs or symptoms of disease occur through the stage of virus dissemination. Thus, the incubation period (the time between exposure to virus and onset of disease) extends from the time of implantation through the phase of dissemination, ending when virus replication in the target organs causes disease. Occasionally, mild fever and malaise occur during viremia, but they often are transient and have little diagnostic value.

The incubation period tends to be brief (1 to 3 days) in infections in which virus travels only a short distance to reach the target organ (i.e., in infections in which disease is due to virus replication at the portal of entry). Conversely, incubation periods in generalized infections are longer because of the stepwise fashion by which the virus moves through the body before reaching the target organs. Other factors also may influence the incubation period. Generalized infections produced by togaviruses may have an unexpectedly short incubation period because of direct intravascular injection (insect bite) of a rapidly multiplying virus. The mechanisms governing the long incubation period (months to years) of persistent infections are poorly understood. The persistently infected cell is often not lysed, or lysis is delayed. In addition, disease may result from a late immune reaction to viral antigen (e.g., arenaviruses in rodents), from unknown mechanisms in slow viral infections during which no immune response has been detected (as in the scrapie–kuru group), or mutation in the host genetic material resulting in cellular transformation and cancer.

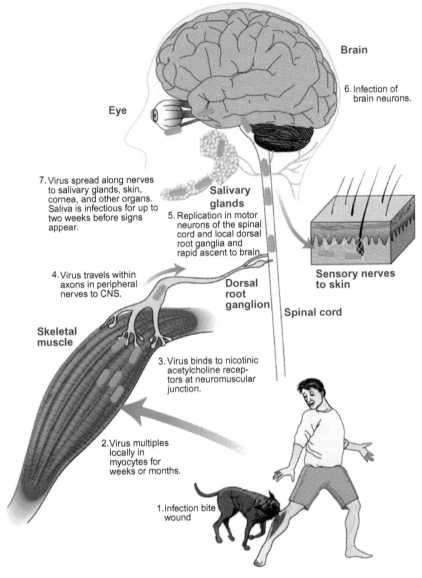

FIGURE 1.4 Virus spread through nerves during a generalized infection. Numbers indicate sequence of events.

MULTIPLICATION IN TARGET ORGANS

Virus replication in the target organ resembles replication at other body sites except that (1) the target organ in systemic infections is usually reached late during the stepwise progression of virus through the body, and (2) clinical disease originates there. At each step of virus progression through the body, the local recovery mechanisms (local body defenses, including interferon, local inflammation, and local immunity) are activated. Thus, when the target organ is infected, the previously infected sites may have reached various stages of recovery. Figure 1.2 illustrates this staging of infection and recovery in different tissues during a spreading surface infection. Circulating interferon and immune responses probably account for the termination of viremia, but these responses may be too late to prevent seeding of virus into the target organ and into sites of shedding. Nevertheless, these systemic defenses can diffuse in various degrees into target organs and thereby help retard virus replication and disease.

Depending on the balance between virus and host defenses, virus multiplication in the target organ may be sufficient to produce dysfunction manifested by disease or death. Additional constitutional disease such as fever and malaise may result from diffusion of toxic products of virus replication and cell necrosis, as well as from release of lymphokines and other inflammatory mediators. Release of leukotriene C4 during respiratory infection may cause bronchospasm. Viral antigens also may participate in immune reactions, leading to disease manifestations. In addition, impairment of leukocytes and immunosuppression by some viruses may cause secondary bacterial infection.

SHEDDING OF VIRUS

Because of the diversity of viruses, virtually every possible site of shedding is utilized (Table 1.2); however, the most frequent sites are the respiratory and alimentary tracts. Blood and lymph are sites of shedding for the arboviruses, since biting insects become infected by this route. HIV is shed in blood and semen. Milk is a site of shedding for viruses such as some RNA tumor viruses (retroviruses) and cytomegalovirus (a herpesvirus). Several viruses (e.g., cytomegaloviruses) are shed simultaneously from the urinary tract and other sites more commonly associated with shedding. The genital tract is a common site of shedding for herpesvirus type 2 and may be the route through which the virus is transmitted to sexual partners or the fetus. Saliva is the primary source of shedding for rabies virus. Cytomegalovirus is also shed from these last two sites. Finally, viruses such as tumor viruses that are integrated into the DNA of host cells can be shed through germ cells.

CONGENITAL INFECTIONS

Infection of the fetus is a special case of infection in a target organ. The factors that determine whether a target organ is infected also apply to the fetus, but the fetus presents additional variables. The immune and interferon systems of the very young fetus are immature. This immaturity, coupled with the partial placental barrier to transfer of maternal immunity and interferon, deprive the very young fetus of important defense mechanisms. Another variable is the high vulnerability to disruption of the rapidly developing fetal organs, especially during the first trimester of pregnancy. Furthermore, susceptibility to virus replication may be modulated by the undifferentiated state of the fetal cells and by hormonal changes during pregnancy. Although virus multiplication in the fetus may lead to congenital anomalies or fetal death, the mother may have only a mild or inapparent infection.

To cause congenital anomalies, virus must reach the fetus and multiply in it, thereby causing maldeveloped organs. Generally, virus reaches the fetus during maternal viremia by infecting or passing through the placenta to the fetal circulation and then to fetal target organs. Sufficient virus multiplication may disrupt development of fetal organs, especially during their rapid development (the first trimester of pregnancy). Although many viruses occasionally cause congenital anomalies, cytomegalovirus and rubella virus are the most common offenders. Virus shedding by the congenitally infected newborn infant may occur as a result of persistence of the virus infection at sites of shedding.

NK CELLS IN HEPATITIS C VIRUS INFECTION

Roughly 170 million people worldwide suffer from chronic hepatitis C virus (HCV) infection, a condition caused by an enveloped single-stranded RNA virus of the Flaviviridae family.[1,2] Complications frequently arise from persistent HCV infection, with liver cirrhosis and hepatocellular carcinoma occurring in approximately 25% and 1%–5% of cases, respectively. Although progression to chronic disease occurs in the majority of infected individuals, about one-fourth of de novo HCV infections are cleared during the acute phase. Resolved infection is characterized by the presence of HCV antibodies in the absence of markers of active viral replication, such as HCV RNA. Viral clearance is thought to rely largely on a broad, potent, and prolonged host cellular immune response.[3–5] Accordingly, defective T cell immunity is strongly associated with viral persistence.[6] No vaccine is currently available to prevent HCV infection, yet the rate of sustained virological responses to treatment has recently significantly increased with the administration of HCV protease inhibitors in addition to the conventional combination of pegylated INF-α and ribavirin.[7] In individuals who spontaneously clear HCV infection, viral control occurs within the first few months of infection. Before the onset of the adaptive immune response, innate immune effector cells, such as NK and NKT cells, are thought to release IFN-γ, which is directly responsible for the noncytopathic inhibition of HCV replication.[8–11] IFN-γ-mediated clearance of the virus might be more important than direct cytolysis of HCV-infected hepatocytes by NK cells, as nearly all hepatocytes become infected and their elimination would lead to extensive liver damage. Type III IFN, such as IFN-λ, has received much attention recently, because not only does this cytokine inhibit HCV replication in vitro,[12] but specific polymorphisms located in the encoding gene, IL28B, are strongly associated with HCV clearance, response to therapy, and disease outcome.[10,13–16] Although the mechanisms underlying IFN-λ-mediated eradication of HCV replication in vivo remain to be determined, it is possible that this cytokine plays a crucial role in modulating NK cell responses to HCV, similarly to IFN-α.[12,17]

NK cells constitute 30% of resident lymphocytes in the normal liver, which is higher than their representation in the peripheral blood, and percentages of NK cells in HCV-infected livers can reach as high as 90%.[17,18] Compared to peripheral blood NK cells, NK cells in healthy livers are characterized by a decreased ability to perform their cytotoxic and immunoregulatory functions, a functional state that might be maintained by high expression of the inhibitory NKG2A receptor on NK cells, and an increased local production of the immunosuppressive cytokine IL-10.[19,20] These features are required to avoid immunopathology of the liver, in which tolerogenic conditions have to be maintained to avoid inflammation in response to gut-derived antigens.

CONCLUSIONS

An increasing body of data suggests that NK cells play a critical role in the control of many viral diseases. Recent studies use a combination of high-throughput "omics" technologies, including genomics, transcriptomics, epigenomics, proteomics, metabolomics, interactomics, and bioinformatics. Omics research has launched the era of molecular medicine. Application of omics in molecular medicine research provides multidimensional analytical approach that reveals molecular pathological portraits. It provides a good deal of biological information and new insights into the gene, protein, and metabolite profiles during various stages of disease. The recent developments in screening omics technologies have allowed the discovery of combinatorial biomarkers.[21] Omics analysis may be translated into practice for risk stratification, early detection, diagnosis, biomarker identification, treatment selection, prognostication, and the monitoring for recurrence.[22]

References

1. Finn WG. Diagnostic pathology and laboratory medicine in the age of "omics": a paper from the 2006 William Beaumont Hospital Symposium on Molecular Pathology. *J Mol Diagn* 2007;**9**:431−6.
2. Hamacher M, Herberg F, Ueffing M, et al. Seven successful years of Omics research: the Human Brain Proteome Project within the National German Research Network (NGFN). *Proteomics* 2008;**8**:1116−17.
3. Keusch GT. What do -omics mean for the science and policy of the nutritional sciences? *Am J Clin Nutr* 2006;**83**:S520−2.
4. Nicholson JK. Reviewers peering from under a pile of omics data. *Nature* 2006;**440**:992.
5. Choo QL, Kuo G, Weiner AJ, Overby LR, Bradley DW, Houghton M. Isolation of a cDNA clone derived from a blood-borne non-A, non-B viral hepatitis genome. *Science* 1989;**244**:359−62.
6. Lavanchy D. The global burden of hepatitis C. *Liver Int* 2009;**29**(Suppl. 1):74−81.
7. Day CL, Lauer GM, Robbins GK, McGovern B, Wurcel AG, et al. Broad specificity of virus-specific CD4 + T-helper-cell responses in resolved hepatitis C virus infection. *J Virol* 2002;**76**:12584−95.
8. Lauer GM, Ouchi K, Chung RT, Nguyen TN, Day CL, et al. Comprehensive analysis of CD8 + -T-cell responses against hepatitis C virus reveals multiple unpredicted specificities. *J Virol* 2002;**76**:6104−13.
9. Rauch A, Kutalik Z, Descombes P, Cai T, Di Iulio J, et al. Genetic variation in IL28B is associated with chronic hepatitis C and treatment failure: a genome-wide association study. *Gastroenterology* 2010;**138**:1338−45.
10. Doherty DG, O'Farrelly C. Innate and adaptive lymphoid cells in the human liver. *Immunol Rev* 2000;**74**:5−20.
11. Lassen MG, Lukens JR, Dolina JS, Brown MG, Hahn YS. Intrahepatic IL-10 maintains NKG2A + Ly49 − liver NK cells in a functionally hyporesponsive state. *J Immunol* 2010;**184**:2693−701.
12. Grakoui A, Shoukry NH, Woollard DJ, Han JH, Hanson HL, et al. HCV persistence and immune evasion in the absence of memory T cell help. *Science* 2003;**302**:659−62.
13. Ulsenheimer A, Gerlach JT, Gruener NH, Jung MC, Schirren CA, et al. Detection of functionally altered hepatitis C virus-specific CD4 T cells in acute and chronic hepatitis C. *Hepatology* 2003;**37**:1189−98.
14. Welsch C, Jesudian A, Zeuzem S, Jacobson I. New direct-acting antiviral agents for the treatment of hepatitis C virus infection and perspectives. *Gut* 2012;**61**(Suppl. 1): i36−46.
15. Guidotti LG, Chisari FV. Immunobiology and pathogenesis of viral hepatitis. *Annu Rev Pathol Mech Dis* 2006;**1**:23−61.
16. Marcello T, Grakoui A, Barba-Spaeth G, Machlin ES, Kotenko SV, et al. Interferons α and λ inhibit hepatitis C virus replication with distinct signal transduction and gene regulation kinetics. *Gastroenterology* 2006;**131**:1887−98.
17. Grebely J, Petoumenos K, Hellard M, Matthews GV, Suppiah V, et al. Potential role for interleukin-28B genotype in treatment decision-making in recent hepatitis C virus infection. *Hepatology* 2010;**52**:1216−24.

18. Shi FD, Ljunggren HG, La Cava A, Van Kaer L. Organ-specific features of natural killer cells. *Nat Rev Immunol* 2011;**11**:658−71.
19. Tillmann HL, Thompson AJ, Patel K, Wiese M, Tenckhoff H, et al. A polymorphism near IL28B is associated with spontaneous clearance of acute hepatitis C virus and jaundice. *Gastroenterology* 2010;**139**:1586−92.
20. Thomas DL, Thio CL, Martin MP, Qi Y, Ge D, et al. Genetic variation in IL28B and spontaneous clearance of hepatitis C virus. *Nature* 2009;**461**:798−801.
21. Cho WC. Cancer biomarkers (an overview). In: Hayat EM, editor. *Methods of cancer diagnosis, therapy and prognosis.* Netherlands: Springer; 2010.
22. Cho WC. Cancer biomarker discovery: the contribution of "omics". *BIOforum Eur* 2007;**11**:35−7.

Further Reading

Albrecht T, Boldogh I, Fons M, et al. Cell activation signals and the pathogenesis of human cytomegalovirus. *Intervirology* 1990;**31**:68.

Coen DM. Acyclovir-resistant, pathogenic herpesviruses. *Trends Microbiol* 1994;**2**:481.

Fields BN. How do viruses cause different diseases? *J Am Med Assoc* 1983;**250**:1754.

Grieder FB, Davis NL, Aronson JF, et al. Specific restrictions in the progression of Venezuelan equine encephalitis virus-induced disease resulting from single amino acid changes in glycoproteins. *Virology* 1995;**206**:994.

Singh IP, Chopra AK, Coppenhaver DH, et al. Vertebrate brains contain a broadly active antiviral substance. *Antiviral Res* 1995;**27**:375.

Strayer DS, Laybourne KA, Heard HK. Determinants of the ability of malignant fibroma virus to induce immune dysfunction and tumor dissemination in vivo. *Microb Pathos* 1990;**9**:173.

Wold WE, Hermiston TW, Tollefson AE. Adenovirus proteins that subvert host defenses. *Trends Microbiol* 1994;**2**:437.

2

Challenges in Molecular Pathology

The challenges are many: New and rapidly changing technology including molecular diagnostics; outsourcing of laboratory testing; capability of instantaneously transferring digital images around the world; and medical decisions based on economics, often with little input from pathologists.

Because the practice of pathology and laboratory medicine evolves rapidly, laboratory medical directors must constantly introduce new tests and services and continue to provide consistent, reliable results for existing tests. Innovations in laboratory medicine are frequently introduced, and the number of commercial vendors of test kits and reagents increases yearly. These innovations, however, may pose barriers to standardization and integration of laboratories and to interpretation of results generated by different laboratories. We propose a practical framework for medical directors to address the seemingly contradictory challenges of standardizing and integrating while simultaneously providing the flexibility to introduce innovations. We recommend initiating standardization first, then integration, while maintaining flexibility for innovation. As organizations strive to create effective processes to enhance value, the role of the laboratory medical director will become critical in resolving the natural tension between standardization/ integration and innovation in laboratory medicine and pathology (Hernandez JS, Jan 2010).

The pathologist has an increasingly central role in the management of cancer patients in the era of personalized oncology. Molecular diagnostic and genomic applications are rapidly penetrating the daily practice of the pathologist as the list of actionable genetic alterations in solid and hematologic malignancies continues to expand. At the same time, a paradigm shift in the diagnostic approach for inherited genetic diseases, infectious diseases, and pharmacogenetics is unfolding. As a result, a plethora of clinical genomic applications is being rapidly implemented in diagnostic molecular pathology laboratories as we move closer to the anticipated reality of "precision medicine."

Sequencing of the first human genome took over 10 years and cost more than $2 billion.[1] Current massively parallel next-generation methods allow a whole genome to be sequenced in weeks at costs under $10,000.[2] Pathologists, as the directors of clinical laboratories, have the expertise to effectively translate genomic technology to patient care. To play this important role pathologists must be trained in genomic methods and result interpretation. This chapter provides evidence demonstrating the need for genomic pathology education, addresses the progress to date of several educational initiatives, and suggests possible ways to improve future training. Much of molecular pathology involves testing for single gene variants (e.g., BRCA (BReast CAncer)). For the purpose of this chapter, genomics refers to analysis of large portions of the genome with a single "test." Aside from the whole genome, only gene-coding regions (exome) or expressed genes (transcriptome) can be sequenced. Chip-based testing, as well as other approaches, can be utilized in the analysis of hundreds of genes, millions of single-nucleotide polymorphisms (SNPs) or copy number variation across the genome.

Genomic testing is being incorporated into almost all areas of medicine. In oncology, genomic analysis of tumors has already led to personalized chemotherapy.

In addition to whole-genome sequencing, gene panels are becoming more commonly used in a variety of cancers. For breast cancer, both a 21-gene and a 70-gene assay performed on tumor samples are commercially available to provide information regarding risk of recurrence and possible need for chemotherapy.[3] A 167-gene assay has also been developed to help determine appropriate management of cytologically indeterminate thyroid nodules.[4] A 13-gene panel of oncogenes has been used to guide pharmacologic management of cancer patients. In a prospective study of salivary duct carcinoma cases, the assay influenced treatment decisions in six of eight patients tested.[5]

Genomics applications are not limited to disease state and are increasingly being offered to healthy individuals. Using a sample of the mother's blood, cell-free DNA is isolated and sequenced and the amount of representation from each chromosome is quantified. For example, an excess of chromosome 21 DNA is consistent with Down syndrome in the fetus. Recent head-to-head studies have also shown that chromosomal microarrays compare favorably to standard karyotyping in regard to prenatal diagnosis and determining abnormalities associated with stillbirth.[6,7]

Genomic testing has also been performed on healthy individuals outside the setting of pregnancy. In transfusion medicine, high-throughput assays have been developed to determine the blood group antigen genotypes of healthy donors.[8] This genotyping will allow better donor—recipient matching and identification of donors with rare variants for which classic serologic methods are of limited utility.

In addition to sequencing human genomes, NGS methods are being applied to microbiologic testing. During the 2011 *E. coli* (Escherichia coli) outbreak in Europe, the entire sequence of the causative organism was determined in a less than a week.[9] During a recent tuberculosis outbreak in Canada, whole-genome sequencing of 32 isolates led to the determination of the outbreak epidemiology when traditional methods failed.[10]

Pathologists are in a unique position to assist in translating genomic technology to clinical care. Pathologists already direct the laboratories offering single gene testing and have the expertise in ensuring accurate and precise results. As the authors of the aforementioned study involving detection of a cryptic *PML-RAR* fusion transcript wrote, "to fully use this potentially transformative technology to make informed clinical decisions, standards will have to be developed that allow for CLIA-College of American Pathologists certification of whole-genome sequencing."[11]

Almost all specimens used for genomic testing will pass through the pathology laboratory. In anatomic pathology, a pathologist must first determine that there is a malignant process before sending for assays that determine prognosis or potential chemotherapy regimens in a given neoplastic disease. In addition, the pathologist must also ensure that an appropriate sample is sent. Determining the type of processing (fresh versus frozen or formalin-fixed) and the portion of the specimen to analyze are crucial in providing accurate results.[12] In clinical pathology, whether in the blood bank, microbiology, hematology, or molecular pathology laboratories, pathologists have access to samples for genomic analysis. Furthermore, pathologists are already versed in incorporating genetic data into pathology reports that enable other clinicians to understand the results and act appropriately.

Given the experience and training of pathologists and clinical laboratorians in sample preparation, assay validation and quality control, one can argue that without pathologists overseeing genomic testing, there is the potential for patient harm. As evidence of such potential danger, in 2009, a direct to consumer (DTC) genomic testing company mixed up samples, leading to clients receiving incorrect results suggesting risk for a variety of diseases.[13]

Commercially offered DTC genomic tests typically use gene chips to study over a million SNPs. Some SNPs are associated with increased risk of disease based on genome wide association studies (GWAS)[14] that use a case control design to determine SNPs associated with a specific disease or trait. The results from GWAS, however, are meant to be used on a population basis and not to determine individual risk. The previously mentioned whole-genome sequencing studies on healthy individuals for the assessment of sudden cardiac death and diabetes also used GWAS data to determine disease susceptibility.[15,16] As noted by the authors of one of these studies, when a patient has multiple risk factors for a disease (e.g., diet, smoking status, medication use, genetic variants), currently "no methods exist for statistical integration of such conditionally dependent risks."[15]

Pathologists are well versed in many of the statistical issues that arise in the setting of genomic testing.[17] For example, a test with very high test specificity (>99 %) may still have a low positive predictive value if the prevalence of the disease in the population tested is very low. This issue is compounded considering that most genomic tests are made up of many individual "tests" (e.g., a multigene panel) which increases the risk of false-positive results.[18] In the genomic era, pathologists' familiarity with issues related to statistics, accuracy, precision, and quality control will be vitally important.

Given the above, pathologists need to be centrally involved in translating genomic methods to patient care. As genomic testing will affect all areas of medicine, however, pathologists will need to collaborate with other specialists such as genetic counselors and medical geneticists. In a pilot study, pathologists developed a workflow for tumor analysis consisting of sample processing, sequencing and result validation.[2] While the authors "anticipate that the molecular genetics and pathology communities will move high-throughput sequencing toward CLIA certification, which will ultimately reduce costs and improve turnaround time," they also describe the formation of a "genomic" tumor board consisting of oncologists, medical geneticists, ethicists as well as pathologists.

Routine molecular diagnostic determinations of tumor specimens in the pathology laboratory have been performed since the late 1990s and concerned mainly classification of tumors, clonality determinations and tests such as short tandem repeat analysis to select patients for referral to clinical geneticists.

GENERAL OVERVIEW OF MOLECULAR APPLICATIONS IN PATHOLOGY

The identification of mutations or chromosomal rearrangements that are characteristic for disease entities can assist the pathologist in the differential diagnosis of these entities.

The identification of specific molecular characteristics may guide therapy. Genetic aberrations can discriminate if morphological similar or asynchronous tumors in one patient represent one or two entities or not, e.g., whether a secondary tumor is indeed an independent tumor or a metastasis of a primary.[19,14]

The observation that some genetic aberrations make tumor cells dependent on or "addicted to" a gene product or cellular pathway has powered the development of drugs that specifically target these aberrations allowing treatment based on the genetic makeup of a tumor, also called precision medicine.[20] At present there are several genetic changes leading to targetable proteins. Examples are overexpression of ErbB2 (HER2) due to *ERBB2* amplification in, e.g., breast cancer, and treatment with trastuzumab (Herceptin)[21] and activating *KIT* and *PDGFRA* mutations in gastrointestinal stromal tumors as targets for the TKIs.[22,23]

TECHNICAL OBSTACLES FOR THE MOLECULAR DIAGNOSTIC INDUSTRY AND IN THE PATHOLOGY LABORATORY

The efforts of The Cancer Genome Atlas (TCGA) initiative have led to a still growing body of information on acquired somatic genomic changes in different cancer genomes.[3] Due to the fast increase of available targeted therapies as well, the TCGA efforts rapidly result in a growing demand for routine molecular tumor diagnostics and screening for actionable mutations in a wide variety of tumor types. To offer patients the best treatment options for a certain tumor, diagnostic tests should be reliable, reproducible, of sufficient high sensitivity, and able to investigate all potential targets with the constrains of limited amount of tissue, time, and budget. These criteria for comprehensive molecular testing require permanent development of new assays, awareness of their potentials and drawbacks, continuous quality assessment to improve testing of diagnostic tissues, consciousness of budget and costs and clinical demands such as turnaround time. Apart from these issues there are tissue and technological challenges as well.

TECHNOLOGICAL CHALLENGES IN MOLECULAR ASSAYS

To detect the various genomic DNA alterations in the tumor cells including point mutations, large insertions and deletions, complex indels, genomic rearrangements, MSI, and promoter methylation, a diversity of methods has been developed for daily routine pathology molecular diagnostics. It can be anticipated that in the era of precision medicine the number of molecular markers, which need to be assessed, will steadily increase per sample. The challenge for the diagnostic laboratory is to select high-performing technological methodologies that enable reliable detection of all mutations requested, at a high sensitivity, with a limited amount of tissue (biopsies, cytological preparations), within short turnaround times and at low costs.

MUTATION DETECTION IN PRECISION MEDICINE

Applied technologies in molecular diagnostics should allow fast implementation of new tests for actionable targets to be able to offer optimal patient care. The need for this is illustrated by the recent trial on treatment of metastatic colorectal cancer, showing that besides *KRAS* exon 2 mutations, another 17% of colon cancers of patients that do not respond to anti-*EGFR* treatment harbor mutations in *KRAS* exon 3 and 4 and *NRAS* exon 2, 3, and 4.[6] Importantly, when using the described low throughput assays, these extra analyses require more material and overall costs and an organized testing pipeline.

FDA (Food and Drug Administration)-approved or CE (Certification)-marked tests suggest a high reliability in clinical testing. However, although the tests themselves may be sensitive, work properly and are standardized, these tests might not cover all clinically relevant mutations. For example, the FDA-approved COBAS *BRAF* mutation test is particularly developed for detection of BRAF p.V600E and may also detect p.V600K and p.V600D mutations albeit less reliable. However, in approximately 25% of the melanomas, clinically relevant *BRAF* codon 600 mutations other than p.V600E occur.[5] Using the COBAS *BRAF* mutation test results in lack of detection of other codon 600 mutations, which withholds patients from appropriate treatment. Although it can be assumed that the laboratories are aware of these shortcomings they still can pass external quality assessment, as long as these laboratories indicate the shortcomings of the test in their standard operating procedure (SOP). It is questionable whether this procedure should be considered as sufficiently high quality and competent patient care.

For diagnostic molecular pathology, whole-genome sequencing is not yet affordable, requires too much DNA, and still has a long turnaround time. At present, there are few options to perform comprehensive analysis for precision medicine, including the OncoCarta panels of bioscience and targeted NGS approaches. The OncoCarta panels are multiplexed PCR systems using a mass spectrometry-based readout for fast screening of more than 200 hotspot mutation sites across 20 cancer genes. Although the method is slightly more sensitive than Sanger sequencing and tests for more mutations, the DNA input to obtain all this information is relatively high ($\sim$ 500 ng), only predefined positions are screened and detected mutations require follow-up conventional sequencing to confirm the presence of the mutation.[1]

NGS-based methods using the Ion Torrent Personal Genome Machine (IT-PGM) from Life Technologies and the MiSeq Benchtop Sequencer from Illumina are now applied for analysis of gene panels for diagnostic purposes.[8,9,24,25] Both platforms use a sequencing-by-synthesis approach, but the underlying sequencing technology differs. The IT-PGM uses semiconductor sequencing detecting hydrogen ion release during base incorporation by DNA polymerase, the Miseq detects emission of fluorescent signal released from labeled nucleotides after incorporation.[12] The sensitivity of NGS is higher than Sanger sequencing. The turnaround time and costs can be competitive with respect to low throughput technologies in centers that have sufficient number of samples. The use of small, dedicated gene panels and efficient loading of the chips for IT-PGM also significantly reduce costs per case. Both IT-PGM and MiSeq systems allow the use of commercially established gene panels as well as custom-designed gene panels for amplicon sequencing. The major benefit of (targeted) NGS is that it uncovers all kinds of mutations in selected genomic regions instead of only mutations at predefined positions. An additional advantage of NGS is that in the same assay mutations and allelic imbalances can be detected, e.g., *EGFR* amplification and loss of heterozygosity by SNP analyses. Currently, a major disadvantage of NGS in implementation in molecular diagnostics is that the data-generating and data-processing technologies are not yet fully developed which regularly leads to equipment and software improvements. Below, we will further discuss these aspects and the consequences for validation of NGS.

DETECTION OF CHROMOSOMAL REARRANGEMENTS: IN SITU HYBRIDIZATION

At present, genomic rearrangements in, e.g., in situ hybridization (ISH) on FFPE material or cytology preparations with commercially available, CE-marked and FDA-approved probes. The advantage of FISH is that it is relatively fast and can be performed semi or fully automated. However, subsequent microscopic analysis of the results is relatively labor intensive. The number of FISH determinations per NSCLC case increases, as apart from *ALK*, also *ROS1* and *RET* rearrangements yield actionable products. Consequently, also the time spent and costs per case expand. Detection of chromosomal rearrangements in, e.g., NSCLC might benefit from an RNA-based sequencing approach that allows simultaneous detection of different chromosomal rearrangements in a limited amount of tissue.

VALIDATION OF COMPREHENSIVE MOLECULAR ASSAYS

Since the number of actionable mutations to be screened for per tumor rapidly increases and the accuracy, speed, and cost enables clinical use of comprehensive molecular assays, there is an urgent need for development of standardization in global validation procedures. Implementation of new technology in the laboratory, e.g., NGS, needs determination of test conditions including DNA input, setup of SOPs, determination of coverage needed, and testing software applications. The desired sensitivity of the test in diagnostic samples determines the read depth, which reflects how often a genomic region has been sequenced. In our centers, we have established NGS assay designs resulting in a read depth per amplicon of $500 \times$ at minimum, which enables accurate detection of low frequency allelic variants. In general, the observed mutation frequency will correlate with the estimated percentage of neoplastic cells, but tumor heterogeneity may account for the presence of low-abundance mutations. A pathologists that is familiar with basic molecular testing should score the percentage of neoplastic cells. The relevance for treatment of mutations present in a low percentage of the malignant cells due to tumor heterogeneity is not clear as yet.[12]

The validation process should assess the entire workflow including the molecular report. The general information that is needed in the report is described by van Krieken et al.[26] In addition, an NGS-test report should include which genes or regions of the genes are investigated, information about the gene coverage, the sensitivity of the detection, and the frequency of the detected mutation. It is highly recommended to evaluate the mutant allele frequency in the context of the percentage of neoplastic cells estimated by the pathologist.

Finally, each high complexity molecular pathology must have a quality management program in place. Below is an example of a well thought plan and program SOP.

QUALITY MANAGEMENT PROGRAM

1.0 Principle/Indications

The quality management program in anatomic pathology involves an active and ongoing surveillance of the quality of day-to-day activities in surgical pathology and cytopathology, including compliance with applicable laws, regulations, facility policies, and the monitoring of diagnostic reports.

2.0 Specimen Requirement/Types

- Gynecological (GYN) cytology
- Non-Gynecological (Non-GYN) cytology
- Biopsy

3.0 Supplies/Equipment/Reagents

Not applicable.

4.0 Instrumentation

Not applicable.

5.0 Calibration

Not applicable.

6.0 Quality Control

Not applicable.

7.0 Environmental Requirements

Not applicable.

8.0 Operating Procedure

- **Peer Review in Surgical Pathology and Cytopathology**
  - All microscopic tissue diagnoses are rendered by a board-certified pathologist, whereas cytopathology diagnoses/interpretations are rendered by a board-certified pathologist or cytopathologist. Negative Pap report interpretations are rendered by ASCP certified and New York State licensed (or elegible, as applicable) cytotechnologists.
  - Each surgical pathology and cytopathology report is reviewed for any errors in identification or completeness by the pathologist and/or cytotechnologist before sign-out. This review occurs at the

time the report is released. Random reviews of completed cases are conducted by the director or designee at his/her discretion.

- Intradepartmental consultations among the staff pathologists occur on a daily basis via consensus conference. Pathologists will bring to consensus interesting cases, unusual findings, difficult cases, etc. for review. In addition, pathologists will bring to consensus first-time malignancies, and cases where clinicians request a second review. Consultations are documented in a log kept on file. Differences of opinion on difficult cases are attempted to be resolved through the consensus conference process. If agreement cannot be reached, these cases are sent out for extradepartmental consultation to appropriate site-specific consultants.

- **Anatomic Pathology Monitors and Quality Indicators (Includes Surgical Pathology and Cytopathology)**
  - All of the following indicators include both surgical pathology and cytopathology and are calculated and reported monthly by the cytology/histology manager as quality indicators.
  - **Turnaround Time**
    - All reports are released by electronic signature into the laboratory information system (LIS). Routine biopsy reports are normally completed within 1 to 2 work days. Cases that need extra fixation time (e.g., Cone/LEEP) or further studies (recuts, consultation or immunohistochemistry) are normally completed within 2 to 3 work days. Non-GYN reports are normally completed within 1 working day, and Pap reports can take anywhere from 1 to 7 (or greater) working days, depending on the test order. Orders for reflex testing usually take the longest, as only final reports are given to clients, unless there are unforeseen circumstances. In other words, if the cytology case includes HPV or other molecular molecular testing, the final report is held till the testing results are completed, so that the final cytology report includes both the cytology interpretation and the results of molecular testing. Note that the cytology interpretation will be performed within the usual timeframe. The results are available for in-house viewing. If further delays are anticipated, either a call to the submitting physician will be made or a preliminary report will be issued, indicating the differential diagnosis and the reason for the delay.
    - Pending case lists (for each case type) are generated by a clerk and reconciled daily. Pending cases that cannot be solved by the clerk are brought to the attention of the cytology/histology manager or designee for reconciliation. Pending lists are signed by the manager and filed in a logbook.

Assessment of Turnaround Time

Responsible party to generate the report	
Responsible party to review the report	Technical laboratory director.
Goal of the report	Ensure that turnaround time in surgical pathology and cytopathology are kept below the established threshold and deviations are monitored.
Standards for report generation	Report should be generated on the first Friday of the month for the previous month's data.
Frequency of the report	Monthly.
Standards for review of reports	Within 48 hours of receipt.
Parameter measured	Average turnaround time for each case type (Non-GYN, Pap, and Surgical). Monitor trends over previous month and year. Annual summary should be generated.
Additional parameter measured	None.
Threshold for normal performance	Non-GYN - 2 days, Pap - 3.75 days, Surgical - 2 days (work days only).
Actions to be taken upon deviation	Prepare plan of correction. Monitor effectiveness of plan of correction.
Documentation of report generation and review	Maintained as QI indicator.

- **Amended Reports**
  - When there is a significant change in patient information or in diagnosis/interpretation (but not limited to either one), a corrected/amended report will be issued and must specify the reason for the amended report. The director and/or cytology/histology manager must be informed of all corrected reports, before release, that involve a change in diagnosis or interpretation.
  - The clinician submitting the specimen will be notified either by direct communication or by fax, as appropriate. This communication is documented in the amended report, accompanied by the date.
  - Disparities in diagnosis or interpretation may be discussed among the pathologists and/or cytotechnologists at the director or manager's discretion.

Assessment of Amended Reports

Responsible party to generate the report	
Responsible party to review the report	Technical laboratory director.
Goal of the report	Ensure that amended report generation in surgical pathology and cytopathology are kept below the established threshold and deviations are monitored.
Standards for report generation	Report should be generated on the first Friday of the month for the previous month's data.
Frequency of the report	Monthly.
Standards for review of reports	Within 48 hours of receipt.
Parameter measured	Percentage of surgical pathology and cytopathology amended reports generated. Monitor trends over previous month and year. Annual summary should be generated.
Additional parameter measured	Clerical vs diagnostic errors.
Threshold for normal performance	0.5%.
Actions to be taken upon deviation	Prepare plan of correction. Monitor effectiveness of plan of correction.
Documentation of report generation and review	Maintained as QI indicator.

• Pathologist Consensus Agreement
Assessment of Pathologist Consensus Agreement

Responsible party to generate the report	
Responsible party to review the report	Technical laboratory director.
Goal of the report	Ensure that monthly percentage of agreement among pathologists is maintained above the established threshold as a measure of concurrence of cytology cases presented to consensus conference.
Standards for report generation	Report should be generated on the first Friday of the month for the previous month's data.
Frequency of the report	Monthly (report to quality management quarterly).

(*Continued*)

Standards for review of reports	Within 48 hours of receipt.
Parameter measured	Percentage of agreement among pathologists on cytology cases presented to consensus conference.
Additional parameter measured	None.
Threshold for normal performance	95%.
Actions to be taken upon deviation	Prepare plan of correction. Monitor effectiveness of plan of correction.
Documentation of report generation and review	Maintained as QI indicator.

- **Extradepartmental Consult Agreement**
  - Cases are occasionally sent out for a second opinion (either by patient/client request, or pathologist request in the case of consensus disagreement). When the consult report is obtained, a supplemental report is issued indicating the findings.

Assessment of Extradepartmental Consult Agreement

Responsible party to generate the report	
Responsible party to review the report	Technical laboratory director.
Goal of the report	Ensure that monthly percentage of diagnostic agreement of in-house and external cytology consult reports is maintained above the established threshold as a measure of concurrence.
Standards for report generation	Report should be generated on the first Friday of the month for the previous month's data.
Frequency of the report	Monthly (report to quality management quarterly).
Standards for review of reports	Within 48 hours of receipt.
Parameter measured	Percentage of agreement among pathologists on cytology cases presented to consensus conference. "Agreement" and "Essential Agreement" will be considered as agreement for this quality indicator.
Additional parameter measured	Agreement; Essential Agreement; Disagreement.
Threshold for normal performance	95%.

- **Cytopathology Monitors and Quality Indicators**
  - All of the following indicators are specific to cytopathology and are calculated and reported monthly by the cytology/histology manager as quality indicators.
  - **Unsatisfactory Rate**

Assessment of Unsatisfactory Rate

Responsible party to generate the report	
Responsible party to review the report	Technical laboratory director.
Goal of the report	Insure that unsatisfactory Pap reports are kept below the established threshold and deviations are monitored.
Standards for report generation	Report should be generated on the first Friday of the month for the previous month's data.
Frequency of the report	Monthly.
Standards for review of reports	Within 48 hours of receipt.
Parameter measured	Percentage of unsatisfactory Pap reports. Measurement will be made for all tests. Monitor trends over previous month and year. Annual summary should be generated.
Additional parameter measured	None.
Threshold for normal performance	0.5%–1.5% (CAP Median for ThinPrep = 1.1%).
Actions to be taken upon deviation,	Prepare plan of correction. Monitor effectiveness of plan of correction.
Documentation of report generation and review	Maintained as QI indicator.

- **% Reports with no Endocervical/Transformation Zone Component**

Assessment of Percentage Reports With No Endocervical/ Transformation Zone Component

Responsible party to generate the report	
Responsible party to review the report	Technical laboratory director.
Goal of the report	Insure that reports lacking endocervical/ transformation zone component are kept below the established threshold and deviations are monitored.

(*Continued*)

Standards for report generation	Report should be generated on the first Friday of the month for the previous month's data.
Frequency of the report	Monthly.
Standards for review of reports	Within 48 hours of receipt.
Parameter measured	Percentage reports lacking endocervical/ transformation zone component. Measurement will be made for all tests. Monitor trends over previous month and year. Annual summary should be generated.
Additional parameter measured	None.
Threshold for normal performance	<8.0%.
Actions to be taken upon deviation	Prepare plan of correction. Monitor effectiveness of plan of correction.
Documentation of report generation & review	Maintained as QI indicator.

• Monthly Pap/HPV HR Correlation
Assessment of Monthly Pap/HPV HR Correlation

Responsible party to generate the report	
Responsible party to review the report	Technical laboratory director.
Goal of the report	Ensure that the distribution of HPV HR positive results correlates to Pap diagnostic categories based on established thresholds and that deviations are monitored.
Standards for report generation	Report should be generated on the first Friday of the month for the previous month's data.
Frequency of the report	Monthly.
Standards for review of reports	Within 48 hours of receipt.
Parameter measured	Percentage of HPV HR positive results within each Pap diagnostic level. Monitor trends over previous month and year. Annual summary should be generated.
Additional parameter measured	None.

Threshold for normal performance	Negative Pap: <10%.
	Reactive/reparative: <30%.
	ASCUS/ASCUSH/AGUS: 45%–70%.
	LSIL: >80%.
	HSIL: >90%.
Actions to be taken upon deviation	Prepare plan of correction. Monitor effectiveness of plan of correction.
Documentation of report generation and review	Maintained as QI indicator

- **ASC/SIL Ratio**

Assessment of ASCUS/SIL Ratio

Responsible party to generate the report	
Responsible party to review the report	Technical laboratory director.
Goal of the report	Insure that monthly ASCUS/SIL ratios fall between the established threshold and deviations are monitored.
Standards for report generation	Report should be generated on the first Friday of the month for the previous month's data.
Frequency of the report	Monthly (report to quality management quarterly).
Standards for review of reports	Within 48 hours of receipt.
Parameter measured	Ratio of cases diagnosed as "Atypical Squamous Cells of Undetermined Significance" over "Squamous Intraepithelial Lesions." Measurement will be made for all tests. Monitor trends over previous month and year. Annual summary should be generated.
Additional parameter measured	None.
Threshold for normal performance	0.7–3.14 (CAP Recommended Median = 2.0).
Actions to be taken upon deviation	Prepare plan of correction. Monitor effectiveness of plan of correction.
Documentation of report generation and review	Maintained as QI indicator.

• Pathologist Referral Rate Comparison to Actual Abnormal Rate
Assessment of Pathologist Referral Rate Comparison to Actual Abnormal Rate

Responsible party to generate the report	
Responsible party to review the report	Technical laboratory director.
Goal of the report	Insure that the difference between cases referred to pathologist and the actual abnormal rate does not exceed the established threshold and deviations are monitored.
Standards for report generation	Report should be generated on the first Friday of the month for the previous month's data.
Frequency of the report	Monthly (report to quality management quarterly).
Standards for review of reports	Within 48 hours of receipt.
Parameter measured	Percentage point difference between cases referred to pathologist and actual abnormal rate. Measurement will be made for all tests. Monitor trends over previous month and year. Annual summary should be generated.
Additional parameter measured	Pathologist referral rate and actual abnormal rate.
Threshold for normal performance	<6.0 percentage points.
Actions to be taken upon deviation	Prepare plan of correction. Monitor effectiveness of plan of correction.
Documentation of report generation and review	Maintained as QI indicator.

• Cytotechnologist Screening Accuracy
Assessment of Cytotechnologist Screening Accuracy

Responsible party to generate the report	
Responsible party to review the report	Technical laboratory director.
Goal of the report	Ensure that the screening accuracies of cytotechnologists in cytopathology are maintained above the established threshold as a measure of the quality of diagnostic interpretation and that deviations are monitored.

Standards for report generation	Report should be generated on the first Friday of the month for the previous month's data.
Frequency of the report	Monthly (report to quality management quarterly).
Standards for review of reports	Within 48 hours of receipt.
Parameter measured	Percentage of cases where the original diagnostic interpretation concurs with a secondary QC screener. Percentage is measured across all cytotechnologists. Monitor trends over previous month and year. Annual summary should be generated.
Additional parameter measured	None.
Threshold for normal performance	95.0%.
Actions to be taken upon deviation	Prepare plan of correction. Monitor effectiveness of plan of correction.
Documentation of report generation and review	Maintained as QI indicator.

- **Paps Received with One Patient Identifier**

Assessment of Paps Received With One Patient Identifier

Responsible party to generate the report	
Responsible party to review the report	Technical laboratory director.
Goal of the report	Ensure that monthly percentage of Paps received with one patient identifier are maintained below the established threshold as a measure of the quality of specimen labeling from client offices.
Standards for report generation	Report should be generated on the first Friday of the month for the previous month's data.
Frequency of the report	Monthly (report to quality management quarterly).
Standards for review of reports	Within 48 hours of receipt.
Parameter measured	Percentage of Paps received with one patient identifier. Measurement will be made across all specimens received. Monitor trends over previous month and year. Annual summary should be generated.
Additional parameter measured	None.

(Continued)

Threshold for normal performance	<1.0%.
Actions to be taken upon deviation	Prepare plan of correction. Monitor effectiveness of plan of correction.
Documentation of report generation and review	Maintained as QI indicator.

- **Surgical Pathology Monitors and Quality Indicators**
  - All of the following indicators are specific to surgical pathology and are calculated and reported monthly by the cytology/histology manager as quality indicators.
  - **Incorrect Entries Into the LIS (Laboratory Information System)**

Assessment of Incorrect Entries Into the LIS

Responsible party to generate the report	
Responsible party to review the report	Technical laboratory director.
Goal of the report	Ensure that ordering/demographic errors in surgical pathology accessioning are kept below the established threshold and deviations are monitored.
Standards for report generation	Report should be generated on the first Friday of the month for the previous month's data.
Frequency of the report.	Monthly.
Standards for review of reports	Within 48 hours of receipt.
Parameter measured	Percentage of surgical pathology orders entered incorrectly into the LIS. Measurement will be made across all orders. Monitor trends over previous month and year. Annual summary should be generated.
Additional parameter measured	None.
Threshold for normal performance	5.0%.
Actions to be taken upon deviation	Prepare plan of correction. Monitor effectiveness of plan of correction.
Documentation of report generation and review	Maintained as QI indicator.

- **Surgical Biopsies Received Without Proper Identification**

Assessment of Surgical Biopsies Received without Proper Identification

Responsible party to generate the report	
Responsible party to review the report	Technical laboratory director.
Goal of the report	Ensure that incidence of irretrievable specimens received lacking proper identification are kept below the established threshold, deviations are monitored and communicated back to the clients through the sales force, and conditions are corrected that lead to inadequately identified specimens.
Standards for report generation	Report should be generated on the first Friday of the month for the previous month's data.
Frequency of the report	Monthly.
Standards for review of reports	Within 48 hours of receipt.
Parameter measured	Percentage of biopsies received without no/ only one/wrong patient identifier. Measurement will be made across all specimens received. Monitor trends over previous month and year. Annual summary should be generated.
Additional parameter measured	None.
Threshold for normal performance	<1.0%.
Actions to be taken upon deviation	Prepare plan of correction. Monitor effectiveness of plan of correction.
Documentation of report generation and review	Maintained as QI indicator.

- **Communications**
  - The submitting physician or designee is notified by telephone for any surgical and/or cytology specimens that are received suboptimally or require clarification. Documentation is kept either in a log or in the comments section of the case in the LIS. If patterns are found from a certain physician location, education on the appropriate submission practices may be initiated by a phone call or a visit by the sales representative.

- The submitting physician is notified by telephone or by FAX of any unexpected findings, including a new positive diagnosis for cancer (with the exception of basal cell carcinoma of skin), the lack of chorionic villi in a product of conception specimen, or an unexpected infectious agent.
- In cytology, correspondence by mail with the gynecologic physicians is initiated by the laboratory to obtain follow-up histological information for correlative review when high-grade SIL or malignant GYN cytological findings are reported. A log is kept to document the correspondence.

- **Correlation with Prior Surgical Pathology and Cytology Material**
  - The LIS has the ability to print out or display the cumulative summary of prior surgical pathology and cytology reports on any given patient. Prior material relevant to the current biopsy is noted in the current report indicating the accession number of the prior case and the given diagnosis, as well as any relevant molecular results (i.e., HPV HR). Review is performed when deemed necessary. Frequently, lack of correlation occurs as a result of sampling error or lack of T-zone in cervical biopsies.
  - In cytology, whenever a GYN high-grade SIL or malignancy is reported, a retrospective review of previously negative and unsatisfactory Pap slides received within the past 5 years is performed and the review is documented. The review is generally performed within 1 week of case sign out. Any discrepancies are noted on the "Five-Year Retro-Review" sheet (see attached). This document is generated after every HSIL and higher diagnosis, regardless if previous cases are available. If significant discrepancies are found that would affect patient care upon the retro-review (i.e., a disease state more serious that was previously reported, and/or abnormal cells of a cell type different than that involved in the current disease state), an amended report is issued and the physician is notified. Retro-review cases are counted as one manually screened slide if a cytotechnologist is performing the review.

- **Circulation of Diagnostic Material**
  - In-house pathologists are permitted to borrow slides for internal slide reviews. The slides will be pulled by the clerk and the pathologist will return the slides after review.
  - In the case of extradepartmental consultation requests by the physician or by the patient, the request is signed either by the submitting physician on the case or by the patient. The slides or recuts are then pulled with the report and with all the necessary paperwork and given to the director or designee for review. The selected slides will be xeroxed and kept in the file with the rest of

the paperwork. If the case has only one significant slide, the slide is usually not permitted to leave the department. Immunohistochemistry slides are sent when necessary.

- For single cytology slides in the file (example: Pap smears), an acknowledgment letter is faxed to the cytopathologist (reviewer) for signature, accepting responsibility for the safe return of the slide following examination.
- The transcriptionist/clerk will follow up periodically on slides that have not been returned in a timely manner with follow-up phone calls, faxes, and/or letters. Documentation of correspondence is maintained in the pathology department.

- **Extradepartmental Consultations**
  - Extradepartmental consultations are usually requested by the submitting physician or by the patient. A pathologist reviews every case that goes out and issues a supplemental report when the result of the consultation is received. A log is kept on the send-outs, including the patient name, case #, number of slides forwarding address, and date sent/returned.
  - If original slides (H&E, IHC, special stains, cytology slides) are sent, the case will be flagged and the clerk will follow up with the institution if slides are not returned promptly.
  - Extradepartmental slides submitted for consultation are accessioned and reported like a routine specimen received by the laboratory, including issuing a formal report to be sent to the submitting physician. The original material is returned promptly. If the slides are recuts and the case is of interest, a request may be sent to the institution to ask for permission to retain the slides.
  - Dermpath cases, specifically melanocytic lesions and neoplasms, are sent to a Dermatopathology lab for processing and diagnosis. The cases are accessioned as a Dermatopathology report; the resulting diagnostic report from the Dermpath lab is attached to the in-house report and sent to the submitting physician by courier and electronically (if applicable). A copy of the Dermpath report is filed with the surg (surgical) path (pathology) case and kept in the laboratory file.

- **Pathologist Competency**
  - All new pathologists are given a correlation study to include a representative sample of retrospective cases routinely reviewed at the institution. Any discrepancies are reviewed by an in-house pathologist and the newly hired pathologist, discussed and documented. Based on the findings and discussion, an assessment is made on whether or not the new pathologist is fit for employment.

- **Cytotechnologist Competency**
  - New cytotechnologists are given an entrance exam before being hired. This serves as the initial competency. Ninety percent compliance is required to pass (one-step changes acceptable, as long as abnormal cases are not called negative and negative cases are not called abnormal). The format and cases of the test provided are at the manager's discretion (see attached "Cytology Entrance Exam"). Upon hiring, 100% of their work is rescreened on their first day, followed by 50% the next day. The cytotechnologist must not miss a low-grade SIL or higher during this period nor miss more than one ASCUS/ASCUSH/AGUS case. It is at the discretion of the manager/pathologist whether or not to do further monitoring or not hire the employee at this point. If the cytotechnologist is hired, the New York State Department of Health is notified within 1 week of the cytotechnologist's start date. The state is also notified when a cytotechnologist is terminated within 1 week of the cytotechnologist's termination.
  - A review of cytotechnologists' errors is performed and documented on the "Cytotechnologist Misses Log" (see attached). At the end of the month, screener scores (see attached "Screener's Monthly Scores") are obtained, based on deductions taken from discrepancies noted via QC (QC score) and pathologist reviews (diagnosis score) (see attached "Quality Control Gradings"). Each screener starts with a score of 100 for both quality control and diagnosis scores, and deductions accumulated from each discrepancy. These deductions vary depending on the number of Paps screened per month by the individual cytotechnologist, as indicated on the "Quality Control Gradings" sheet. This is to ensure that a fair evaluation is done on the screener. Cytotechnologists who work full time are expected to miss a higher quantity of cases than those who work part time or on a per diem basis. The exception is with significant discrepancies, which include two-step changes (see attached "Two-Step Miss Log"). The same deductions apply to these cases no matter how many slides are screened per month.
  - Remedial actions: Any remedial actions taken against a cytotechnologist are at the discretion of the manager and/or director. The following guidelines are used but exceptions can be made depending on the circumstances:
    - If there is continuous over or under calling by the cytotechnologist, the manager and/or director will speak to the cytotechnologist about the individual circumstance. This may or may not be documented in writing. If warranted, a performance improvement program (PIP) may be initiated.

- Missing a low-grade lesion: The cytotechnologist is given the case to rescreen to verify that he/she noted that the diagnostic cells were missed. Fifty percent of the cytotechnologist's work is rescreened by a qualified cytotechnologist either the same day (if possible) or the next day that he/she is scheduled to work. The discrepancy is documented in the "Two-Step Miss Log" and "Cytotechnologist Misses Log." Documentation is provided on the "Quality Control Rescreen Record" sheet obtained and signed by the original screener that he/she reviewed the case. It is expected that these occurrences do not occur regularly. Remedial actions may take place at the discretion of the manager or director such as decreasing workload or continual monitoring at 50% rescreen if necessary. A 10% deduction is taken from the screener score regardless of how many slides the cytotechnologist screens for that particular month. Note: If a low-grade lesion is missed at the diagnosis level (in the event a case was given to a pathologist originally as negative or reactive), the discrepancy is documented, but remedial action is generally not necessary.
- Missing a high-grade lesion: The cytotechnologist is given the case to rescreen to verify that he/she noted that the diagnostic cells were missed. Fifty percent of the cytotechnologist's work is rescreened by a qualified cytotechnologist the either the same day (if possible) or the next day that he/she is scheduled to work. The discrepancy is documented in the "Two-Step Miss Log" and "Cytotechnologist Misses Log." It is expected that these occurrences do not occur regularly. Remedial actions may take place at the discretion of the manager or director such as decreasing workload or continual monitoring at 50% rescreen if necessary. This cannot be a repeated problem, however. *If this should occur during the first month of initial employment, the cytotechnologist is terminated. If three occurrences occur during a 1-year period by the same person, the cytotechnologist is also terminated.* A 20% deduction is taken from the screener score regardless of how many slides the cytotechnologist screens for that particular month. Note: If a high-grade lesion is missed at the diagnosis level (in the event a case was given to a pathologist originally as "Negative" or "Reactive"), the discrepancy is documented, but remedial action is generally not necessary.
- Missing a carcinoma: The same as a high-grade lesion applies to missing a carcinoma, except that a 35% deduction is taken regardless of how many slides the cytotechnologist screens for that particular month, and 100% of the cytotechnologist's work is rescreened by a qualified cytotechnologist the either the same day (if possible) or the next day that he/she is scheduled to

work. Additional remedial actions may be warranted in these instances at the discretion of the manager or director.

- Other two-step Changes: Other quality control or diagnosis misses that include two-step changes (e.g., ASCUS to HGSIL) are also documented on the same log sheets as mentioned above. HGSIL to ASC-H and ASC-H to HGSIL are not considered two-step changes. Deductions are taken as indicated on the "Quality Control Gradings" sheet.
- Note: In the event that a discrepancy is found that was not picked up by the ThinPrep Imaging System or FocalPoint GS Imaging System, it is recorded on the "Quality Control Rescreen Record" that it was an Imager error and the cytotechnologist will not require remedial action.
- Workload standards: Every cytotechnologist, as well as the manager is responsible for verifying that workload numbers do not exceed regulations from New York State. If employed elsewhere, cytotechnologists are to provide documentation of outside screening at other laboratories to verify that totals for the day do not exceed the maximum allowed.
- Cytotechnologists participate in College of American Pathologists (CAP) proficiency testing, which is provided once a year. Those who are unable to attend the scheduled test date are to provide documentation of passing the test taken at another laboratory. Documentation is on file in the pathology department and the QA department. If a cytotechnologist fails their first attempt, retesting is scheduled and must pass the second time or the cytotechnologist is terminated. This corrective action is documented. Proficiency testing attestation pages are signed by the laboratory director and the individual performing the testing.
- Formal competency assessments are given to all cytotechnologists every 6 months minimum, unless further monitoring is required (e.g., new instrumentation such as the ThinPrep Imaging System and FocalPoint GS Imaging System require quarterly monitoring for the first year). See attached "Cytology Competency Assessment" for the forms in use. Competencies are signed by the employee, manager, and director. A number of factors contribute to a cytotechnologist's competency assessment, and discretion is given to the manager on what items to weigh higher than others. A number (1 to 4) is given to each item on the competency assessment based on performance for the period. The total is averaged out, certain items weighed more than others, at the end of the competency form and an overall score is obtained based on those numbers. Copies of competencies are kept in the QA coordinator's office.

- **Histotechnologist, Grosser, and Cytoprep Technician Competency**
  - Histotechnologists and Cytoprep Technicians are evaluated on a yearly basis using the attached competency assessment forms, with the exception of their first year of employment, where they are evaluated every 6 months, and annually thereafter. Grossing personnel are evaluated in addition by the supervising pathologist on an annual basis. Copies of competencies are kept in the QA coordinator's office.
  - Histotechnologists participate in the CAP HistoQIP (includes histology and immunohistochemistry) program. Since there are no proficiency tests available in surgical pathology, these are considered alternative assessments. A minimum grade of "2" on the evaluation form is considered a passing score. If any scores come back less than "2," corrective action is documented and may involve a documented discussion of the case(s), performing an internal proficiency on additional sample types of the same nature, or other means. Documentation of HISTQIP is kept in the "Continuing Education" binders.
- **Continuing Education and Performance Improvement**
  - The laboratory is enrolled in the following programs.
    - CAP PIP in surgical pathology: All sign-out pathologists participate in this educational program. CAP interlaboratory comparison program in gynecologic cytopathology and non-gynecologic cytopathology: All available cytotechnologists participate in these educational programs. CAP interlaboratory comparison programs are provided for cytotechnologists to complete throughout the year, usually on a quarterly basis. Answers are sent to CAP through fax or electronically and copies of the responses are kept. Copies of cytotechnologist answers are kept in the continuing education binder. For the CAP non-GYN cytopathology program, CAP NGC slidesets are considered an alternative assessment for proficiency testing. Grades of 80% or greater are considered a passing score. All NGC slideset answer sheets are graded and distributed back to the cytotechnologists and pathologists, but these are only considered alternative assessments for those cytotechnologists routinely prescreening Non-GYN cases, and only for pathologists routinely performing final sign-out of these cases. For all other cytotechnologists, these are considered educational activities. The laboratory chooses results based on a consensus of all cytotechnologist and pathologist result forms. Corrective action is documented accordingly, which may include a laboratory alternative assessment of only non-GYN cases, documented discussions about the cases, or other means.

- CAP gynecologic cytology PT program: All cytotechnologists and pathologists signing out cytology cases are required to take the yearly proficiency test, either on site or elsewhere, and must achieve a passing score. If a cytotechnologist fails their first attempt, retesting is scheduled and must pass the second time or the cytotechnologist is terminated. This corrective action is documented. Proficiency testing attestation pages are signed by the laboratory director and the individual performing the testing.
- CAP HistoQIP (includes histology and immunohistochemistry): Performed by available histotechnologists and are considered alternative assessments (see above).
- ASCP cytopathology and histology teleconferences: The laboratory enrolls in spring and fall teleconferences specific to cytology and histology. All available staff is encouraged to attend.
- Interesting cases/cytotechnologist consensus: Additional interesting cases are provided for cytotechnologists to review at the manager's discretion for continuing education purposes. These may or may not include non-GYN cases, where the same alternative assessment criteria apply as in the above bullet on CAP interlaboratory comparison programs. On occasion, the manager may distribute slides for a consensus among cytotechnologists, where cases where there are significant discrepancies among them as a whole are reviewed by the pathologists for their feedback.
- A minimum of 24 hours of continuing education is required for each cytotechnologist. If unable to perform the minimum education, documentation is kept from education performed at other laboratories in the continuing education binder. Cytopreparatory and histology personnel are required to obtain a minimum of 12 credits per year through attending ASCP teleconferences or other means.
- **Training**
  - All staff is required to have proper training in methods and equipment. Training is performed by equipment vendors and other staff members. Documentation is required in the form of a certificate or other means of training documentation (e.g., training checklist). Documentation is kept in the QA coordinator's office and/or pathology laboratory.
- **Cytology Quality Control**
  - A minimum of 10% of negative GYN cytology cases (ThinPrep and conventional slides) are rescreened by a qualified cytotechnologist, and a minimum of 15% of SurePath FocalPoint GS cases are

rescreened. Qualified cytotechnologists entail those that have a minimum of 6 years' experience and have approval by the New York State Department of Health to perform quality control rescreening. High-risk patients with negative diagnoses are included in this rescreen. Results of primary screens and rescreens are documented with any changes in diagnoses on the "Cytology Quality Control Rescreen Record" (see attached). High risk cases include those with previous abnormalities, abnormal bleeding, and any other clinical information that would warrant a case to be rescreened. These are identified through a patient history match when a case is opened (history screen opens automatically for cytotechnologists when a case is opened). Additionally, the following are always submitted for rescreen:

- Endometrial cells found in women over 40 years of age (QC cytotechnologist sends to pathologist review for final confirmation)
- No endocervical/transformation zone component
- Unsatisfactory cases
  - Note: In the event that a case for a patient with a previous consecutive unsatisfactory result comes in, the QC screener will refer the case to the cytology manager. When the history screen is viewed, previous unsatisfactory results are indicated by an empty diagnosis box. The QC screener must perform this extra step before screening an unsatisfactory case. The manager will then request specimen processing to prepare a second slide in an attempt to improve squamous cellularity for adequacy reassessment before sign out.
- Cases with known current positive HPV results
  - Note: The primary screener will only send to QC cases diagnosed as "Negative" where the HPV "Detected" result is available. For those cases where the HPV result is reported as "Detected" after the primary screener provides an interpretation as "Negative," the pathology secretary will pull the slides and list them on a separate "Cytology Quality Control Rescreen Record of Cases with Positive HPV Results" log (see below), and give them to a qualified secondary QC screener.
  - Glandular cells in a patient with a vaginal source and/or total hysterectomy
- The WindoPath LIS prevents the sign out of quality control cases before rescreening is complete. All cases sent for quality control rescreening are placed in a separate queue (Needs Rescreen) and will not be released until signed out by a secondary cytotechnologist.

- Cytotechnologists will place their slides queued for QC in a separate tray, along with the "Cytology Quality Rescreen Record" below, and list the case numbers, number of slides for each case, and the reason for QC on the sheet. A qualified secondary cytotechnologist will review these cases and either sign out as negative, or flag for pathologist review if warranted.
- **Cytotechnologist Dotting Protocol**
  - Primary screening cytotechnologists will use blue permanent marking pens.
  - Secondary (QC) screening cytotechnologists will use green permanent marking pens.
  - Cytotechnologists will mark areas and/or cell(s) of interest with a permanent marker with either a hook, L-shape, circle (for most significant area/cell(s) of interest), or a single dot above and below the areas/cell(s) of interest.
  - For GYN cytology cases, these include, but are not limited to the following.
    - Endocervical/transformation zone component
    - Endometrial cells (if patient is over 40 years old)
    - Abnormal cells
    - Glandular cells in a patient with a vaginal source and/or total hysterectomy
    - Organisms (e.g., fungus, trichomonas, actinomyces)
    - Viral changes (e.g., herpes)
  - For Non-GYN cytology cases, elements will be marked based on the specimen source (e.g., urothelial cells, blood, crystals in urine; glandular cells, abnormal cells in a rectal Pap).
- **GYN Cytology Abnormal Case Review**
  - For GYN cytology cases, each cytotechnologist places his/her abnormal slides, including reactive/reparative changes, in a separate folder with a referral sheet for the pathologist to review before sign out (see attached "Cytology Case Referral and Correlation"). Cells of interest are marked with a permanent marker on the slide. Copies of these forms are kept in the cytotechnologists' binders and/or in a folder designated for the cytotechnologist to review for feedback.
- **Non-GYN Cytology Case Review**
  - All Non-GYN cytology cases are submitted for pathologist review for final sign-out. The WindoPath LIS prevents the sign-out of Non-GYN cytology cases by a cytotechnologist. The same referral sheet that is used for GYN cytology abnormal case review is used for this purpose.

- **Statistics**
  - For cytology, statistics are provided on a monthly basis on abnormal referral rates, ASC/SIL ratio, and diagnostic category for each cytotechnologist. These documents are kept in the "Cytology Statistics by Tech" binder. Additionally, yearly statistics are provided on the number of cytology samples sent and are updated on a monthly basis in the "Cytology Yearly Statistics" binder. Statistics on the number of specimens by type of preparation (ThinPrep, SurePath, Conventional) and source (multiple Non-GYN sources) are also provided. Data on the numbers of cases and percentages of each interpretive category are also provided, as well as additional statistical data as required in the annual cytopathology report.
  - For surgical pathology, annual statistics are kept regarding the number of surgical cases, slides, blocks, special stains, and immunohistochemistry slides made.
- **Review and Implementation of Policies and Procedures**
  - All policies and procedures in anatomic pathology are reviewed once per year by the current medical laboratory director or designee. Paper or electronic signature review is documented for each policy and procedure, and is evident on a separate sheet attached to each policy/procedure.
  - Substantial revisions are reviewed and approved by the director before implementation, and the review is documented as above.
  - If a new director is appointed, he/she will ensure that appropriate documentation and review of the policy and procedure manuals is performed.
  - Any new or revised policy or methodology will be conveyed to the appropriate personnel by the manager, and if education or training is indicated, this will be also be arranged by the manager. Knowledge and training of the specific testing activities for each employee is documented by a sign-off sheet that is attached to each policy/procedure and/or in the front of the procedure manual. All staff requires yearly sign-off of all procedures.
  - Discontinued procedures are retained for a minimum of 2 years.
- **Specimen Handling**
  - **Specimen Collection Requirements**
    - All primary specimen containers must be labeled with at least two unique identifiers at the time of receipt. All slides received must be labeled with at least a patient name, preferably with a second unique identifier. Examples of identifiers include but are not limited to: patient full name, date of birth, requisition #, patient ID (PID).

- A requisition form must accompany all specimens, with the following information:
  - Patient full name
  - Date of birth
  - Sex
  - Submitting physician's name (or designated professional personnel)
  - *Source of specimen
  - Collection date
  - Clinical information, where appropriate
  - If information is missing from the requisition or specimen container, or needs verification, a transcriptionist or client services will contact the physician's office to resolve the issue. The correct information is documented either on a log, the requisition form, and/or in the LIS. The name of the person providing the correct information is also documented.
  - *If no source is provided for a GYN case, client services will attempt to retrieve the source from the client. If there is no response within 48 hours, the following note will be entered: "Cervical (source by default, verification attempts unsuccessful)."
- **Specimen Rejection Criteria**
  - Clinical labs exercise the option to reject specimens and refuse testing on specimens for the following reasons:
    - Specimen and test request was not ordered and/or written by a licensed physician/professional personnel.
    - No patient name on requisition form and no name on the specimen container or submitted slides.
    - The specimen has been labeled, collected, transported, handled, or stored in a manner to render the specimen unsatisfactory for testing in such a way that the results of such testing may yield erroneous, misleading or inconclusive results (e.g., specimens left unfixed for an extended period of time, specimens received with contamination from an unknown source or on the outside surface of the container, mislabeled, unlabeled, or mismatched specimens with accompanied requisition, unknown specimen source, broken slides, etc.).
    - The specimen submitted is inappropriate for the test requested (e.g., a fixed specimen for chromosomal analysis).
    - When a specimen presents with one or more of the above, the specimen is put aside and the referring physician or the office is immediately notified by phone. The documentation is indicated on the req (requisition) slip and/or in the LIS, with the date and the name of the office personnel notified. If the issue cannot be resolved, the specimen is returned to the client.

- **Special Handling for Pap Specimens Received with One Patient Identifier**
  - For all specimens other than surgical biopsies, those that are received with one form of identification on the specimen container (e.g., patient's name and no other unique identifier) will be processed, but will include a comment in the "Source" section of the WindoPath report. The comment will say "Specimen received with one patient identifier," and will be entered at the time the case is accessioned.
  - On a monthly basis, the pathology manager will compile a spreadsheet listing the clients that are deficient with providing two forms of patient identification on specimen containers submitted to the laboratory. The spreadsheet will then be sent to the sales division, where representatives will address the issue with specific clients. This is also maintained as a quality indicator.
- **Special Considerations for Surgical Pathology Specimens Received with Either No Identification, One Patient Identifier, or Misidentification**
  - Special considerations may be taken when irretrievable specimens are received lacking all appropriate patient identification on the specimen container(s) in the interest of providing superior patient care. In the event an irretrievable specimen is received, such as a surgical biopsy, where there is one patient identifier, no identification on the specimen container, or a misidentification, the following procedure will be followed:
    - The case will be accessioned into the SLAB LIS using the patient name that is on the requisition with the "Test in Question" case flag attached.
    - Once uploaded into the LIS, comments will be typed in the "comment" field in the visit tab of the accessioning window, accurately describing the deficiency in identifying the specimen.

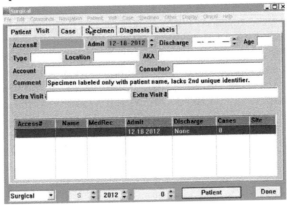

- The specimen container with accompanying requisition is then forwarded to the pathology manager or designee for further investigation and resolution.
- The office will be notified of the deficiency in identifying the specimen and given two options. Each case will be handled on an individual basis depending on the circumstances. Options given are described below.
  - The client may have the specimen returned to their office via courier to be properly identified. The courier will hand deliver the specimen to the office personnel, wait for the specimen to be properly identified (i.e., add second unique patient identifier), and bring the specimen back to the laboratory for processing. Risks associated with this option include the rare possibility of losing the specimen in transit as well as delays in reporting.
  - Note: This option is highly discouraged, and is only used in extreme circumstances, with pathologist or medical director approval.
- The client may have us process the specimen in the interest of providing patient care without delay. If this option is chosen, the specimen will be processed. However, a written attestation from the submitting physician will be required acknowledging the deficiency in identifying the specimen correctly upon collection. The attestation must also include a statement that the said specimen can be positively identified through alternate means. Examples include, but are not limited to: (1) it was the only biopsy sent on that collection date, (2) the biopsy in question is the only one from a specific site taken on that collection date. Alternate identifiers not listed in one (1) and two (2) above must be approved by the medical director.
  - The surgical pathology report will not be signed out until the attestation is received back from the submitting physician. Additionally, the following disclaimer will be added to the surgical pathology report: **"Specimen received with no/only one/ wrong patient identifier. Attestation for an irretrievable specimen is obtained from the ordering physician and the specimen is analyzed. However, results should be interpreted in this context."**
  - Data are tracked monthly and communicated to the sales force through a quality indicator (Assessment of Surgical Biopsies Received Without Proper Identification) so that feedback and/or in-services can be provided to specific clients in the event trends are observed.

9.0 Maintenance

- Department equipment is maintained as per maintenance log sheets and protocols. Service reports are kept as well in the event of preventative maintenance or repair in the operator manuals or attached to the maintenance logs. All new instrumentation is validated before implementation as per manufacturer's protocols and/or in-house established validation procedures. Maintenance records are kept indefinitely for the life of the instrument.
- All reagents must be stored as per manufacturer's instructions. Outdated/expired reagents are not used. If a reagent has no expiration date, one will be assigned, based on known stability, frequency of use, storage conditions, and risk of deterioration. Stains and solutions are filtered (ThinPrep Nuclear Stain only) and/or changed at appropriate intervals and documented on corresponding maintenance charts. All staining dishes and reservoirs are labeled appropriately. Lot numbers are also documented for all reagents on corresponding charts, to include the open date (date put in use), and expiration date.

10.0 Calculations

Not applicable.

11.0 Result Reporting

Not applicable.

12.0 Procedural Notes

Not applicable.

13.0 Limitations

Not applicable.

14.0 Instrumentation Downtime

Not applicable.

15.0 References

Not applicable.

References

1. Beadling C, Heinrich MC, Warrick A, et al. Multiplex mutation screening by mass spectrometry evaluation of 820 cases from a personalized cancer medicine registry. *J Mol Diagn* 2011;**13**:504–13.

2. Bellon E, Ligtenberg MJ, Tejpar S, et al. External quality assessment for KRAS testing is needed: setup of a European program and report of the first joined regional quality assessment rounds. *Oncologist* 2011;**16**:467–78.

3. Cancer Genome Atlas Research. Comprehensive genomic characterization defines human glioblastoma genes and core pathways. *Nature* 2008;**455**:1061–8.

4. Chapman PB, Hauschild A, Robert C, et al. Improved survival with vemurafenib in melanoma with BRAF V600E mutation. *N Engl J Med* 2011;**364**:2507–16.

5. da Rocha Dias S, Salmonson T, van Zwieten-Boot B, et al. The European Medicines Agency review of vemurafenib (Zelboraf(R)) for the treatment of adult patients with BRAF V600 mutation-positive unresectable or metastatic melanoma: summary of the scientific assessment of the Committee for Medicinal Products for Human Use. *Eur J Cancer* 2013;**49**:1654–61.

6. Douillard JY, Oliner KS, Siena S, et al. Panitumumab-FOLFOX4 treatment and RAS mutations in colorectal cancer. *N Engl J Med* 2013;**369**:1023–34.

7. Emile JF, Tisserand J, Bergougnoux L, et al. Improvement of the quality of BRAF testing in melanomas with nationwide external quality assessment, for the BRAF EQA group. *BMC Cancer* 2013;**13**:472.

8. Endris V, Penzel R, Warth A, et al. Molecular diagnostic profiling of lung cancer specimens with a semiconductor-based massive parallel sequencing approach: feasibility, costs, and performance compared with conventional sequencing. *J Mol Diagn* 2013;**15**:765–75.

9. Geurts-Giele WR, Dirkx-van der Velden AW, Bartalits NM, et al. Molecular diagnostics of a single multifocal non-small cell lung cancer case using targeted next generation sequencing. *Virchows Arch* 2013;**462**:249–54.

10. Geurts-Giele WR, Leenen CH, Dubbink HJ, et al. Somatic aberrations of mismatch repair genes as a cause of microsatellite-instable cancers. *J Pathol* 2014;**234**(4):548–59.

11. Bovee JV, Hogendoorn PC. Molecular pathology of sarcomas: concepts and clinical implications. *Virchows Arch* 2010;**456**:193–9.

12. Ulahannan D, Kovac MB, Mulholland PJ, et al. Technical and implementation issues in using next-generation sequencing of cancers in clinical practice. *Br J Cancer* 2013;**109**:827–35.

13. van den Bent MJ, Hartmann C, Preusser M, et al. Interlaboratory comparison of IDH mutation detection. *J Neurooncol* 2013;**112**:173–8.

14. van der Sijp JR, van Meerbeeck JP, Maat AP, et al. Determination of the molecular relationship between multiple tumors within one patient is of clinical importance. *J Clin Oncol* 2002;**20**:1105–14.

15. Felsberg J, Malzkorn B, Bujan B, et al. Molecular diagnostics of glioma – results of the first interlaboratory comparison of MGMT promoter methylation testing at twenty-three academic centers in Germany, Austria and the Netherlands. *Clin. Neuropathol* 2013;**32**:414–15.

16. Gargis AS, Kalman L, Berry MW, et al. Assuring the quality of next-generation sequencing in clinical laboratory practice. *Nat Biotechnol* 2012;**30**:1033–6.

17. van Krieken JH, Jung A, Kirchner T, et al. KRAS mutation testing for predicting response to anti-EGFR therapy for colorectal carcinoma: proposal for an European quality assurance program. *Virchows Arch* 2008;**453**:417–31.

18. van Krieken JH, Jansen C, Hebeda KM, Groenen PJ. Biomarkers as disease definition: mantle cell lymphoma as an example. *Proteomics Clin Appl* 2010;**4**:922–5.

19. Blokx WA, Lesterhuis WJ, Andriessen MP, et al. CDKN2A (INK4A-ARF) mutation analysis to distinguish cutaneous melanoma metastasis from a second primary melanoma. *Am J Surg Pathol* 2007;**31**:637−41.
20. Weinstein IB. Cancer. Addiction to oncogenes−the Achilles heal of cancer. *Science* 2002;**297**:63−4.
21. Piccart-Gebhart MJ, Procter M, Leyland-Jones B, et al. Trastuzumab after adjuvant chemotherapy in HER2-positive breast cancer. *N Engl J Med* 2005;**353**:1659−72.
22. Joensuu H, Roberts PJ, Sarlomo-Rikala M, et al. Effect of the tyrosine kinase inhibitor STI571 in a patient with a metastatic gastrointestinal stromal tumor. *N Engl J Med* 2001;**344**:1052−6.
23. Lasota J, Miettinen M. Clinical significance of oncogenic KIT and PDGFRA mutations in gastrointestinal stromal tumours. *Histopathology* 2008;**53**:245−66.
24. McCourt CM, McArt DG, Mills K, et al. Validation of next generation sequencing technologies in comparison to current diagnostic gold standards for BRAF, EGFR and KRAS mutational analysis. *PloS One* 2013;**8**:e69604.
25. Tops BBJ, Normanno N, Kurth H, Amato E, Mafficini A, Rieber N, Le Corre D, Rachiglio AM, Reiman A, Sheils O, Noppen C, Lacroix L, Cree IA, Scarpa A, Ligtenberg MJL, Laurent-Puig P. Development of a semi-conductor sequencing-based panel for genotyping of colon and lung cancer by the Onconetwork consortium. BMC Cancer. 2015;15:26.
26. van Krieken JH, Siebers AG, Normanno N. European consensus conference for external quality assessment in molecular pathology. *Ann Oncol* 2013;**24**:1958−63.

Further Reading

Nowak F, Soria JC, Calvo F. Tumour molecular profiling for deciding therapy−the French initiative. *Nat Rev Clin Oncol* 2012;**9**:479−86.
Nowak F, Calvo F, Soria JC. Europe does it better: molecular testing across a national health care system-the French example. *Am Soc Clin Oncol Educ Book* 2013;332−7.
Raymaekers M, Bakkus M, Boone E, et al. Reflections and proposals to assure quality in molecular diagnostics. *Acta Clin Belg* 2011;**66**:33−41.

3

Review of Clinical Human Medical Genetics

The human DNA sequence is highly polymorphic; for a typical gene, different people have different specific sequences (or alleles) for that gene. As a result, for the typical protein, different people have different levels of activity in that protein. If the activity of a protein is significantly greater or less than the level of activity that is seen in the typical person, that individual will have a greater or lesser susceptibility to the diseases the protein's function influences than the typical person does. Whether a high-activity or low-activity gene allele represents a risk-increasing allele or a risk-decreasing allele depends on the specific function the protein performs. While some risk-increasing alleles are relatively common, and some increase the individual's risk for the associated disease dramatically, most risk-increasing alleles are relatively rare, and most only increase the individual's risk for the associated disease by a small amount.

Below is a short introduction of the main factors involved in medical genetics.

DEOXYRIBONUCLEIC ACID (DNA)

Overview

- DNA is a large nucleic acid polymer arranged in chromosomes for storage, expression, and transmission of genetic information.
  - The genetic information is encoded by a sequence of nucleotides.
  - Components of DNA.
  - Bases are molecules containing carbon–nitrogen rings in DNA.
  - Purines: Adenine (A) and guanine (G) have two joined carbon–nitrogen rings.

- Pyrimidines: Thymine (T) and cytosine (C) have one carbon–nitrogen ring.
- Nucleoside is made up of a five-carbon sugar (deoxyribose) and a base.
- Deoxyribose is the same sugar found in RNA, but with oxygen removed from the 2′ carbon position.
- Nucleotide is made up of a phosphate group, a pentose sugar (deoxyribose), and a nitrogenous base (Fig. 3.1).

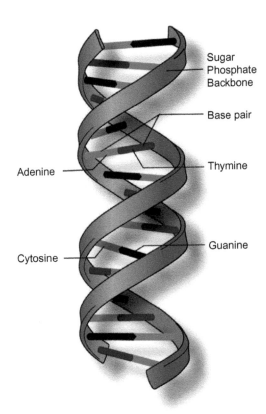

Deoxyribonucleic acid (DNA)

FIGURE 3.1   There are four bases in DNA: Adenine (A), guanine (G), thymine (T), and cytosine (C). Adenine and guanine are purines and thymine and cytosine are pyrimidines. Deoxyribose is the sugar in DNA. The carbon atoms are numbered as indicated. Note there is no oxygen on site 2 of deoxyribose. A nucleoside molecule is composed of a base and deoxyribose. When a phosphate group is added to nucleoside, the complex becomes a nucleotide. Nucleotides are the basic building blocks of DNA.

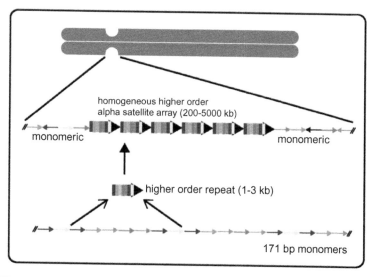

FIGURE 3.2   Example of a megasatellite DNA.

- The phosphodiester bond
  - The phosphate group is bond to the nucleoside at the hydroxyl group of the 5′ carbon atom of deoxyribose.
  - Phosphodiester bonds are strong covalent bonds between phosphate groups connecting the 5′ carbon of one deoxyribose to the 3′ carbon of the next deoxyribose of the adjacent nucleotide nucleotide (Fig. 3.2).
  - The phosphodiester bond determines DNA chain polarity (ends designated as either 5′ or 3′).
  - DNA sequence refers to the order of the nucleotides in a DNA strand, which code for unique sets of genetic information, both proteins and regulatory segments.

Types of DNAs

- Single copy DNA is a specific DNA sequence that is present only once in the genome.
- Repetitive DNA is a DNA segment with a specific DNA sequence that is repeated multiple times in the genome.
- Moderately repetitive DNA refers to 10–105 copies of the sequence per genome.
- Moderate repeated DNA is found primarily in noncoding sequences.
- Highly repetitive DNA describes DNA sequence present in greater than 105 copies per genome.

- Highly repeated DNA is found primarily in centromere and telomere regions as tandem repeats.
- NA has two DNA chains; one is oriented 5'.

The DNA strands are synthesized and read out by RNA polymerase in the 5'–3' direction. The purine or pyrimidine attached to each deoxyribose projects into the center of the helix. Base A pairs with T and a G pairs with C through hydrogen bonds in the central axis.

- These segments of DNA are satellite DNA because of the experimental observation that they often form a minor satellite band near the major centrifugation fraction when DNA is separated by density gradient.
- Clusters of such repeats are scattered on many chromosomes. Each variant is an allele that is inherited codominantly.
- Megasatellite DNAs are tandem repeat DNA segments with a length greater than 1000 bp (1 kbp) repeated 50–400 times.
- Satellite DNAs comprise about 15% of human DNA. The repeated sequence ranges from 5 to 170 bp and the complex is about 100 kbp in length.
- Minisatellite DNAs are repeated sequences ranging from 14 to 500 bp in length. The repeat complex is 0.1–20 kbp in length. Minisatellite DNA is present in telomere region.

Overview

- What is RNA?
  - RNA is a single-stranded nucleic acid polymer consisting of nucleotide monomers (Fig. 3.3).
  - The five-carbon sugar in RNA is ribose (contains a 3' hydroxyl group) instead of deoxyribose.
  - Bases in RNA are A (adenine), G (guanine), C (cytosine), and U (uracil), which takes the place of T (thymine) in DNA.
  - RNA folds back on itself to form hair pin or loop structures via intramolecular hydrogen bonds.
- What is protein?
  - Proteins are chains of amino acids joined by peptide bonds (Fig. 3.4).
  - The peptide bond forms when the carboxyl group of one amino acid residue is joined to the amino group of the next amino acid residue.
- Synthesis of RNA in cells.
- In transcription a DNA sequence is enzymatically copied by an RNA polymerase in a process analogous to DNA chain duplication.

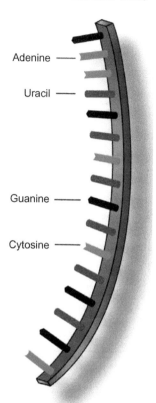

Adenine ——

Uracil ——

Guanine ——

Cytosine ——

Ribonucleic acid (RNA)

FIGURE 3.3   Ribonucleic acid structure.

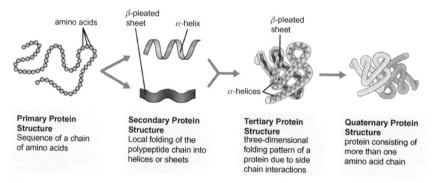

amino acids   β-pleated sheet   α-helix   β-pleated sheet

α-helices

Primary Protein Structure
Sequence of a chain of amino acids

Secondary Protein Structure
Local folding of the polypeptide chain into helices or sheets

Tertiary Protein Structure
three-dimensional folding pattern of a protein due to side chain interactions

Quaternary Protein Structure
protein consisting of more than one amino acid chain

FIGURE 3.4   Protein structures are made up of chains of amino acids joined by peptide bonds.

In RNA transcription, A from DNA template determines U in RNA instead of T.

- RNA polymerases are a group of nucleotidyltransferases that polymerize ribonucleotides in accordance with the information present in DNA.
- RNA polymerase I transcribes genes encoding ribosomal RNA (rRNA).
- RNA polymerase II transcribes genes encoding proteins (mRNA) and certain small nuclear RNAs (snRNA).
- RNA polymerase III transcribes genes encoding transfer RNA (tRNA) and other small RNAs (5SRNA in ribosomes).
- Primase catalyzes the synthesis of the short RNA primers on single-stranded DNA templates used by DNA polymerase to initiate the synthesis of Okazaki fragments on the lagging strand.
- Primase is an essential enzyme in all well-characterized systems of DNA replication because no DNA polymerase can initiate DNA synthesis without an RNA primer.
- The enzyme is required for synthesis of the lagging strand.

CONTEXT OF CLINICAL HUMAN GENETICS

How do the major players (DNA, RNA, proteins) affect our Health? How are medical practitioners using currently available cutting edge technology to improve clinical decisions? Let's see.

The increase in our understanding underlying the biology and mechanisms of disease has spawned a new generation of tests using previously unused "tissue" sources with levels of detection that only a few years ago would have seen inconceivable. Thus, we are now able to identify DNA sequence mutations using whole-genome approaches in single cells isolated from peripheral blood, assess the underlying etiology of tumors from their mutational signatures, and perform methylation and expression analysis with profiles that give prognostic and/or predictive information.

Much of our increased knowledge have been underpinned by platform enablers such as autopsy and tissue banking which have become disciplines of their own, with the emergence of specialty expertise that is needed to provide appropriately collected, processed, and stored samples for molecular interrogation into research. There is emerging data to demonstrate close similarities between tumors of vastly different origins but look, behave, and respond to therapeutic targets in the same manner. This discussion will continue over the coming decade, but it is likely that a combination of conventional and innovative technologies will be used to go from a standard classification system to more of an ontology definition of tumors with all the ancillary information that this provides. A highly thought-provoking and provocative "future scoping" further explores how pathology and the revolution in technology and platform enablers may change the face of pathology across not only the neoplastic diseases but throughout all pathology.

Molecular diagnostics are based on the analysis of biomarkers such DNA, RNA, or protein to identify risk or incidence of disease, determine disease progression (prognostic tests), determine therapy, and/or predict response (predictive or companion diagnostic tests). Microarrays enable high throughput measurements of DNA, RNA, or protein and have contributed vastly to our current research practice. One of the earliest descriptions of the use of "DNA microarrays" or "DNA chips" is probably the study by Augenlicht et al. in 1987 which measured the relative expression of each of 4000 complementary DNA (cDNA) sequences from biopsies of human colonic tissue and in colonic carcinoma cells.[1] A follow-up study focused on 30 cDNA clones in an attempt to compare the expression profiles between two genetic groups from patients at high risk for developing colorectal cancer and normal colonic mucosa in low-risk individuals.[2] The earliest precursors of current gene-expression microarrays were reported in 1995 and 1996 by Schena et al.[3,4] Genomic sequencing arrays, "sequencing by hybridization" (SBH), were first reported in 1992 by Drmanac et al.[5] Shortly after, Drmanac et al. in 1994[6] and 1996[7] reported on newly developed methods for large-scale production of cDNA and genomic DNA microarrays. One particularly pivotal development was the Affymetrix gene-expression array by Lockhart et al. in 1996.[8,9] Comparative genome hybridization arrays (array—CGH or aCGH) were also developed in 1992 to enable high throughput cytogenic analysis in cancer[10] and further developed in 1999 for higher resolution and applied in breast cancer.[11] Protein microarrays, based on reverse-phase method where proteins are spotted onto membranes and detected by antibodies, were not developed until 1999 by Lueking et al.[12] Alternative to the solid surface chips described so far, bead-based microarrays (BeadArray technology) were a later addition to the field which were based on the invention of David Walt and colleagues reported in 1998[13] and developed by Illumina Inc. (founded in 2001). Illumina Inc. was the new competitor of the then microarray-market dominant Affymetrix Inc. (founded in 1992). BeadArrays was initially used for single nucleotide polymorphism (SNP) profiling but later developed for gene-expression profiling in 2004.[14] Since the 1990s, microarrays have developed and expanded considerably to enable high throughput, genome-wide profiling of DNA mutations, copy number variations (CNVs), gene expression (mRNA), proteins, methylation, and microRNA (miRNA). Next-generation sequencing (NGS) methods developed in the late 1990s are now providing the next levels of accuracy, speed, and low cost to employ in molecular profiling of cancer. NGS applies to genome sequencing, transcriptome profiling (RNA-Seq), DNA−protein interactions (ChIP-sequencing), and epigenome characterization.

Early examples of differential molecular profiling include those carried out in melanoma in 1996,[15] and prostate,[16] renal,[17] and breast[18,19] cancers in 1999. Such studies have attracted several reviews, commentaries, and views on the paradigm shift in research where "the hypothesis is there is no hypothesis"[20] and early recognition of the potential of microarrays in drug discovery and response to therapies.[21,22] The feasibility of molecular classification of cancer based solely on gene expression was first demonstrated in leukemia in 1999 based on class prediction methods.[23] Perhaps, the seminal studies by Perou et al. in 2000[24] and Sørlie et al. in 2001[25] were the first to demonstrate the utility of molecular profiling to explain heterogeneity and more importantly the discovery of the association between the distinct molecular profiles and clinical outcomes. The Cancer Genome Atlas (TCGA)[26] and the International Cancer Genome Consortium (ICGC)[27] projects. Continue to expand our understanding of several cancer types at multiple levels of molecular architecture by genome-scale profiling of DNA, RNA, and proteins as well as the integration of such profiles to provide more comprehensive portraits of complex regulatory interactions in cancers. One persistent question remains: how can we translate our findings to benefit patients?

Approved Molecular Medicine Assays in Pathology

In Europe, CE marking for an in vitro diagnostic (IVD) product is required before it can be launched in the market (Directive 98/79/EC). In the United States, pathological tests are regulated by the Food and Drug Administration (FDA) as in vitro diagnostic medical devices (IVDMD) under two main types of applications: 510(k) and the more comprehensive Premarket Approval (PMA). These applications govern pathological tests and related instrumentation used to carry out testing when used to assist in clinical diagnosis/patient management.

In 2013, the FDA published a document "Paving the Way for Personalized Medicine: FDA's role"5 describing how the FDA is responding to regulate and drive the rapid developments in personalized medicine. In 2014, the FDA notified the US Congress regarding laboratory-developed tests (LDTs; such as CLIA-cleared tests)[6] with a draft guidance of framework for regulatory oversight of such tests,[7,8] which are becoming more complex and with higher risk in the new era of "omics." More recently, the Precision Medicine Initiative (PMI) was announced by the US president.[28,29]

During the first stage of development, discovery, biologically and clinically interesting "omics"-based biomarkers need to demonstrate the intended clinical use. The vast majority of "omics"-based molecular profiles arise from cancer patient cohort studies where a statistically significant separation of clinical outcomes of claims and suggestions of clinical utility. Some studies, although limited, take the next leap to illustrate the ability of the "omics"-based profiles as an assay, which may or may not have analytical validity, to stratify some clinical outcomes using independent retrospective cohorts. Even with this effort, this remains to be in the "discovery" phase and should be labeled as clinical validity rather than utility. Clinical utility is achieved if high levels of evidence have been generated to consistently demonstrate that the "omics"-based tests can improve clinical outcomes for the patient when compared to not using the assay.

Genomic studies, such as the TCGA and ICGC projects, are not clinical trials although clinical outcomes such as overall survival or recurrence/metastasis-free survival are recorded for the patients who are receiving the standard treatments for the given cancer. As such, "omics"-profiles or derived assays remain to be limited to prognosis or at best serving as predictive biomarkers for standard therapies (surgery, radiotherapy, or chemotherapy). The genomic tests currently approved for breast cancer are very clear illustration of this nature. Oncotype DX, MammaPrint, and Prosigna were all discovered and based on gene-expression profiling of retrospective breast cancer cohorts.

The Centers for Disease Control and Prevention (CDC) have developed a process for evaluating emerging genetic tests. The CDC-sponsored ACCE Project performs an evaluation that hinges around four aspects of the test: Analytic validity; clinical validity; clinical utility; and the ethical, legal, and social issues related to genetic testing.

The analytic validity of the test refers to whether the test properly measures the phenomenon it is intended to measure. This is often the least controversial aspect of the evaluation. The technologies that are used for DNA testing have wide application, and have not only been subjected to rigorous quality control procedures, but often have withstood at least a moderately stringent test of time and usage. The laboratories that perform the medically useful tests are all certified under the Clinical Laboratory Improvement Amendments of 1988 (CLIA), which requires stringent quality control measures. In addition, the kits that are developed and sold to other laboratories are classified as medical devices, and as such are subject to regulation by the US FDA. There is usually little doubt regarding the analytic validity of the results these laboratories generate.

There is much less information available regarding the probability for error in the newer whole-genome scans that are becoming increasingly available, including those that are offered directly to consumers. Many of the tests that are included in these whole-genome screens have been developed in the laboratory that uses them (laboratory-developed tests, LDTs). While the test is validated in the laboratory that develops it, LDTs are not subject to FDA regulation. The laboratory that developed the test cannot sell it to other laboratories, but it can use the test as part of the service it offers to consumers.

Clinical validity refers to how reliably the result of the test predicts a clinical outcome, such as the individual's risk for developing a disorder or his/her response to a drug. Clinical utility refers to whether the result of the test changes the plan for treating the patient. Tests that detect risk-increasing alleles that have high penetrance are clinically useful, because knowing the individual possesses one of these alleles will often prompt the physician to prescribe an especially rigorous schedule of screening tests, and perhaps other measures that have been reported to detect or prevent the disease. If the risk-increasing allele has low penetrance, however, possessing one risk-increasing allele may increase the individual's overall risk for the disorder to such a small degree that learning that the patient possesses the risk- increasing allele will not change the plan for the patient's treatment.

A genomic test's clinical validity can be subdivided into positive predictive validity (PPV) and negative predictive validity (NPV). A test's PPV is defined as the percentage of people with a positive test result (i.e., who possess the risk-increasing allele) who develop the disorder within a specified time frame. Note that because the genetic and nongenetic factors that contribute to the disease can accumulate over time, the PPV should refer to the probability of developing the disease over a specified time frame (the lifetime risk is often given). The PPV of a genetic test is directly related to the test's level of sensitivity (sensitivity = the proportion of people who have the disorder or who will develop the disorder who had a positive test). There are several reasons why there may be people who develop the disorder despite having had a negative result (or lack of risk-increasing alleles) on the test. For one, the test may have failed to detect a risk-increasing allele that was present. Alternatively, the individual may not possess that particular risk-increasing allele, but may have developed the disorder because he/she possesses risk-increasing alleles in other critical genes, and/or has been exposed to one or more causative nongenetic factors. Finally, the PPV of any genetic test is reduced by anything that reduces the penetrance of the risk-increasing allele. As described earlier, there are a number of reasons for nonpenetrance of a risk-increasing gene allele.

Tests for gene mutations that cause single-gene disorders have excellent clinical validity, because in those cases there are no other causative factors to be considered, and the penetrance of these mutations is essentially 100%.

Clinical utility refers to whether the results of a genetic test will change the plan to treat or manage the disorder. Unfortunately, the fact that a genetic variant contributes to one's risk of developing a multifactorial disorder does not necessarily mean that the test for this genetic variant will have substantial clinical utility. There are many occasions when a new genetic discovery provides important insights into the pathogenesis of that particular disease, but determining the patient's status for the associated genetic polymorphism will not change the way the physician treats the patient.

Because of the number of genetic and nongenetic factors that influence one's risk for the typical multifactorial disorder, most of the risk-increasing gene alleles that contribute to the common multifactorial disorders confer only a small increase in the individual's risk for developing the disorder.

SNPs are Influential Single Nucleotide Polymorphisms

SNPs are merely a single nucleotide position at which one person will have an A, e.g., while another person will have a C, G, or T in the sequence. As of this writing there have been approximately 15 million SNPs reported to exist in the human genome, and SNPs are the genetic polymorphisms that are most commonly used for genetic testing. If the nucleotide substitution causes an amino acid substitution, and the amino acid that gets added into the protein is different enough in electrical charge, polarity or size from the amino acid it is replacing, this may cause the protein to work at an activity level that is significantly higher or lower than the activity level at which most of the isoforms of that protein work. If that protein's function is such that it influences the individual's susceptibility to a multifactorial disorder, the individual with the unusual-activity isoform of the protein will be either more or less susceptible to the disorder than the typical person is.

A SNP test is sometimes named for the DNA nucleotide that is involved, but if the different alleles of the SNP are known to cause different amino acids to be incorporated into the protein, the SNP may be named according to the amino acid substitution that is involved. For example, one of the genetic factors that influence an individual's susceptibility to hereditary hemochromatosis is a SNP in the human hemochromatosis (HFE) gene. Some people have a G at nucleotide number 845 in the HFE gene's coding sequence, while others have an A in that position. At the nucleotide level, this SNP can be symbolized as G845A, or n845G > A, using the letter "n" to indicate that we are describing the SNP at the nucleotide, rather than amino acid, level.

Deletions and Insertions in Human DNA

There are a number of places in the human genome at which some people will possess a certain stretch of nucleotides, while others will not. These polymorphisms are referred to as insertion/deletion polymorphisms (often abbreviated as "indel").

The ribosome reads the mRNA in 3-nucleotide codons, and each codon directs the ribosome to add one amino acid into the growing polypeptide chain. Deletions and insertions in a gene's coding sequence that involve an even multiple of three nucleotides will often result in the deletion or insertion of one or more amino acids from the protein, but will leave the amino acid sequence of the protein normal both before and after the deletion/insertion. Depending on how many amino acids are deleted or added, and exactly where in the protein the deletion/addition occurs, this may or may not change the level of activity in the protein.

Deletions and insertions that lie in the coding sequence of a gene and involve a number of nucleotides that is not evenly divisible by three shift the ribosome's reading frame, and cause the ribosome to read a completely different set of codons. The ribosome will add a certain number of novel amino acids into the polypeptide chain, and sooner or later encounter a STOP codon that causes it to cease adding amino acids and release the polypeptide. In most cases, this will produce a nonfunctional protein.

The human DNA contains a large variety of repeated sequences, ranging from mononucleotide repeats (ex. CCCCCCCC) to repetitions of a 1000 bp motif. There are a few repeated sequence length polymorphisms in coding regions of genes, but most of the repeated sequence length polymorphisms that have been identified as risk-influencing genetic factors lie in the promoter region of their gene.

Although most of the repeat length polymorphisms that are known to contribute to multifactorial disorders involve short repeated sequences like the UGT1A1 dinucleotide repeat, several known functional polymorphisms involve larger repeated sequences. For example, there is an 86 bp repeat polymorphism in intron 2 of the interleukin-1-receptor antagonist (IL-1RA) gene, which encodes a protein that inhibits the inflammatory response. There are five known alleles, ranging from 2 to 6 repeats of the 86 bp sequence. Most people have four repeats of the 86 bp motif at this locus, but some people have only two (this allele is referred to as the IL1RN*2 allele). The IL1RN*2 allele reduces the level of expression of the IL-1RA protein. The IL1RN*2 allele is associated with a poor prognosis in individuals with several chronic inflammatory diseases, including systemic lupus erythematosus, ulcerative colitis and alopecia areata. It has also been reported to be associated with diabetic nephropathy, a chronic hypochlorhydric response to Helicobacter pylori infection and an increased risk for gastric cancer.

Trinucleotide repeats expand during meiosis, whereupon the members of each succeeding generation will have increasingly longer strings of the repeated sequence. In many cases, this leads to the clinical phenomenon of anticipation, in which members of each succeeding generation are affected earlier in life and more severely than members of previous generations. Trinucleotide repeat testing is performed for several disorders, including Fragile X syndrome, Huntington disease, myotonic dystrophy, Friedrich's ataxia, dentatorubropallidoluysian atrophy, spinobulbar muscular atrophy (Kennedy disease), and several forms of *spinocereballar ataxia*. For each disorder, there is a threshold number of repeats of the trinucleotide motif at which the risk for meiotic instability, and therefore rapid expansion from generation to generation, increases.

Short Tandem Repeats are Observed in Certain Types of Cancer

Short tandem repeats such as dinucleotide, trinucleotide, and tetranucleotide repeats are often referred to as microsatellites. The presence of the microsatellite in the DNA sequence can cause the DNA polymerase to slip during DNA replication, and add more or fewer repetitions of the repeated sequence to the newly synthesized DNA strand than it is supposed to. If left uncorrected, this would causes the length of our microsatellite repeats to increase or decrease as we passed them from one generation to the next. Our DNA repair proteins usually correct these DNA replication errors, however. When our DNA repair mechanisms are working properly, microsatellites are stable during meiosis, and rarely change in length from one generation to the next. When our DNA repair mechanisms are not working properly, however, microsatellites will be unstable, not only during meiosis, but during the DNA replication that is involved in mitosis as well. Some have suggested that disruption of the ability to repair genetic abnormalities is an essential step in the progression from the precancerous state to cancer. Mutations in the genes whose proteins are involved in DNA repair can therefore constitute important somatic mutations that contribute to the development of certain types of cancers. The presence of MSI in malignant cells indicates that the ability to repair damaged DNA has been compromised in the tissue being investigated.

The presence of MSI is detected simply by determining the size of the repeated sequence. When MSI is observed in a patient's malignant cells, it is often wise to perform a mutation analysis to search for mutations in genes whose proteins help repair damaged DNA, and referral for genetic counseling is appropriate.

Microsatellites also serve to indicate other important mechanisms for disease. Microsatellites are often highly polymorphic; in fact, many individuals are heterozygous for many microsatellite polymorphisms. SNP array analyses have revealed that patients with disorders as diverse as cancer, mental retardation, and blindness have sometimes long (perhaps several Mb) stretches of contiguous microsatellites for which the affected cells have homozygous genotypes, but the individual's normal cells from another tissue have heterozygous genotypes. This LOH may result from a simple deletion, reduplication after deletion, recombination during mitosis or other mechanisms.

LOH in one or more microsatellites may indicate a deletion that has removed one copy of a gene that lies close to the microsatellite(s). When it comes to influencing the individual's phenotype, some gene alleles are dominant over others; the recessive allele would have relatively low penetrance, because the dominant allele would control the individual's phenotype. If an individual had one allele that was dominant over the other for a particular gene, and the deletion removed the dominant gene allele, this would allow the normally recessive or low-penetrance allele that remained to influence the individual's phenotype more strongly than it usually does. When one finds LOH in one or more microsatellites in a patient who has cancer, it may indicate that the patient has a deletion in his/her DNA, and that the deleted region contains a gene that in turn contains a polymorphism that influences risk for that disease. If the risk-increasing gene allele can be detected, this can provide a means to screen other family members to better estimate their risk for the disorder (Fig. 3.5).

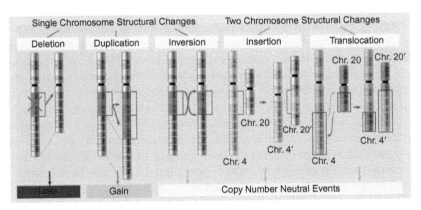

FIGURE 3.5   A schematic representation of types of chromosomal rearrangements.

Chromosome Rearrangements

It is well known that chromosome rearrangements such as transloca-
tions, inversions, duplications and deletions can have sufficiently delete-
rious effects on the individual's metabolism to causes disorders on their
own. Recent studies have demonstrated, however, that chromosome
rearrangements are much more common than we once thought, and
that they are capable of contributing to the development or progression
of certain complex multifactorial disorders as well.

Chromosome rearrangements are especially important in cancer, as
the progression to malignancy is often accompanied by several chromosome rearrangements in transformed cells. For example, it is common to
determine whether a patient with chronic myelogenous leukemia, acute
lymphoblastic leukemia or acute myelogenous leukemia possesses a specific translocation between chromosomes 9 and 22 [t(9;22)(q34;q11)],
commonly called the Philadelphia chromosome, before deciding whether
to prescribe that patient tyrosine kinase inhibitors such as Dasatinib.

Copy Number Variation

It is generally assumed that we have two copies of each gene (except
males' X and Y chromosome genes), but recent research has shown that
many people have deletions and duplications of portions of their DNA
that result in them having greater than or less than two copies of certain
genes (generically referred to as CNVs). One example that has wide
clinical importance is the fact that a small percentage of people have
duplications of a portion of chromosome 22 that result in them having
3–13 potentially functional copies of the cytochrome p450 2D6
(CYP2D6). Fluorescence in situ hybridization assays and microarray
analyses are capable of detecting CNVs.

When we think of gene mutations, we usually think of loss-of-
function mutations, in which the activity of the protein is impaired.
Some gene variants constitute gain-of-function mutations, however. As
described earlier, there are a surprising number of individuals who possess duplications that result in extra functional copies of one or more
genes. In addition, there are many situations in which we cannot predict
the effect of a sequence variation on gene activity, and must directly
measure the gene's level of activity in order to determine the significance of the variant.

Determining the level of activity in a specific gene(s) can help classify
a cancer at the molecular level and guide the choice of treatments. This
may be determined indirectly by detecting extra copies of the gene in
the patient's DNA, or directly by determining the level of the mRNA or
protein in question in the appropriate cells.

In addition to determining the patient's genotypes, personalized medicine can also include tailoring drug therapy to the specific strain of virus or bacterium that is infecting the individual. For example, some strains of the HIV virus infect T cells by using the T cells' surface protein CCR5 to gain entrance. A blood test can be performed to determine whether the patient has been infected with CCR5-tropic HIV-1, and is therefore a candidate for "entry inhibitor" drugs such as maraviroc. DNA sequencing and/or PCR/restriction endonuclease assays can be used to determine the type of pathogen the patient has been infected with.

Somatic Mutations Versus Germline Mutations

Genetic analyses in patients with cancer often must include determining what genetic abnormalities have occurred in the malignant cells themselves. This often necessitates a search for somatic mutations in the malignant cells themselves. Somatic mutations are mutations that arise after fertilization, as the cells are replicating, dividing, and differentiating into their individual cell types. Because somatic mutations arise after fertilization, they only exist in cells that have descended from the cell in which the mutation originally arose. A somatic mutation can drastically alter the metabolism of the cells in which it resides. Because cancer begins with the disruption of metabolism in a single cell, somatic mutations make significant contributions to the development and progression of many cancers. As a cancer progresses, the malignant cells often accumulate gene mutations and chromosome rearrangements that can be used not only to predict the individual's prognosis, but also monitor the individual's response to drugs.

In order to derive the most accurate possible estimate of the individual's susceptibility to a disease, or the best prediction of the individual's response to a treatment, one must combine genetic information, clinical data, family history, and information related to the individual's diet, environment, and lifestyle. The genetic data must include polymorphisms from genes whose proteins influence as many aspects of the disease process or drug's actions as possible, including polymorphisms from genes whose proteins mediate the normal function of the pathways that are affected by the disease or the drug. Genetic information should be used to complement traditional indicators, not replace them, as predictors of disease susceptibility and drug response.

Over the Counter Genetic Testing

The genome-wide SNP screens that are advertised directly to consumers include many tests that are designed to detect risk-increasing alleles that have low penetrance. Critics of personalized medicine testing warn that people who have received the results from a genome-wide SNP screen, but who do not understand the concept of penetrance and the multifactorial nature of complex diseases, may become unnecessarily anxious upon finding out they possess a "risk allele." This is indeed a concern, and it highlights the importance of genetic counseling in the process, even when the process does not require an appointment with a physician.

As the cost of genetic testing declines, physicians and other health-care practitioners will see an increasing number of patients who have obtained information about their genetic status, but do not know how to interpret that information within the framework of their healthcare plan. In this section, we discuss the GWA studies that provide the foundation for these genome-wide SNP screens, and provide background information that will help you explain the limitations of the results of these tests to patients.

As more and more genomes are sequenced, however, it is becoming apparent that the human DNA sequence is so variable that there are many rare variants, and many that have not yet been reported in the literature, that influence different individuals' risks for these diseases. In addition, this is a particularly important concern for tests that assess the individual's status at a site that is not believed to be a functional polymorphism, but instead is believed to lie close to a functional polymorphism.

As the cost of DNA sequencing declines, sequencing will come to replace these site-specific tests as the method of choice for whole-genome screens. Sequencing detects all variants that exist in the DNA, even those that have never been reported before. As a result, it is capable of identifying not only novel mutations in known genes, but also novel genes whose disruption can contribute to the disease.

A good term which is sometimes used to describe the degree to which a risk-increasing allele contributes to a disease is attributable risk. The attributable risk is calculated (Table 3.1) simply by subtracting the frequency of the disease in people without the risk-increasing allele from the frequency of the disease in people with the risk-increasing allele.

SNPs and Functional Polymorphisms

DNA sequence polymorphisms are often referred to as markers, for several reasons. Researchers who discovered the sequence of the human DNA molecule and mapped the position of all the genes on their chromosomes began using the term in the same way cartographers do. Because the sequence of the entire human DNA molecule has been

TABLE 3.1   Calculating Attributable Risk Using a Contingency Table

Attributable Risk (AR)

Contingency (or 2 x 2) Table

	Cases	Controls	Total
Exposed	a	b	a+b
Unexposed	c	d	c+d
Total	a+c	b+d	a+b+c+d

$$AR = I_E - I_U$$
$$= P(D|E) - P(D|U)$$
$$= [a/(a+b)] - [c/(c+d)]$$
$$AR\% = AR * 100$$

published, we now know the exact location of each of these polymorphic sites on its respective chromosome.

Insights Into the Mechanisms for Disease

The frequency with which recombination confounds the interpretation of these tests can be specified as the recombination frequency (Rf) between the linked marker and the critical gene/polymorphism. If a risk-increasing allele is detected at a marker that is linked to a critical gene polymorphism, unless you know the Rf between the tested marker and the critical polymorphism, you don't know how reliable that information is. The higher the Rf is between the marker and the polymorphism, the greater the probability is that the patient possesses the "risk-increasing" allele of the linked marker, but not the true risk-increasing allele of the critical gene polymorphism.

It has been estimated that the entire human genome can be covered by testing 300,000–600,000 properly selected tagging SNPs. This is well within the capacity of current microarray technologies.

With continued development and availability of genetic test offerings, there will be greater need for physicians to help their patients interpret their results and to know when it is appropriate to refer to a genetic specialist. In addition, physicians should be able to understand the process whereby basic research discoveries are translated into clinically useful genetic tests.

References

1. Augenlicht LH, Wahrman MZ, Halsey H, Anderson L, Taylor J, Lipkin M. Expression of cloned sequences in biopsies of human colonic tissue and in colonic carcinoma cells induced to differentiate in vitro. *Cancer Res* 1987;**47**(22):6017−21.
2. Augenlicht LH, Taylor J, Anderson L, Lipkin M. Patterns of gene expression that characterize the colonic mucosa in patients at genetic risk for colonic cancer. *Proc Natl Acad Sci USA* 1991;**88**(8):3286−9.
3. Schena M, Shalon D, Davis RW, Brown PO. Quantitative monitoring of gene expression patterns with a complementary DNA microarray. *Science* 1995;**270**(5235):467−70.
4. Schena M, Shalon D, Heller R, Chai A, Brown PO, Davis RW. Parallel human genome analysis: microarray-based expression monitoring of 1000 genes. *Proc Natl Acad Sci USA* 1996;**93**(20):10614−19.
5. Drmanac R, Drmanac S, Labat I, Crkvenjakov R, Vicentic A, Gemmell A. Sequencing by hybridization: towards an automated sequencing of one million M13 clones arrayed on membranes. *Electrophoresis* 1992;**13**(8):566−73.
6. Drmanac S, Drmanac R. Processing of cDNA and genomic kilobase-size clones for massive screening, mapping and sequencing by hybridization. *Biotechniques* 1994;**17**(2):328−9 332−6.
7. Drmanac S, Stavropoulos NA, Labat I, Vonau J, Hauser B, Soares MB, et al. Gene-representing cDNA clusters defined by hybridization of 57,419 clones from infant brain libraries with short oligonucleotide probes. *Genomics* 1996;**37**(1):29−40 Available from: https://doi.org/10.1006/geno.1996.0517.
8. Lockhart DJ, Dong H, Byrne MC, Follettie MT, Gallo MV, Chee MS, et al. Expression monitoring by hybridization to high- density oligonucleotide arrays. *Nat Biotechnol* 1996;**14**(13):1675−80. Available from: https://doi.org/10.1038/nbt1296-1675.
9. Editorial. To affi... and beyond!. *Nat Genet* 1996;**14**(4):367−70. Available from: https://doi.org/10.1038/ng1296-367.
10. Kallioniemi A, Kallioniemi OP, Sudar D, Rutovitz D, Gray JW, Waldman F, et al. Comparative genomic hybridization for molecular cytogenetic analysis of solid tumors. *Science* 1992;**258**(5083):818−21.
11. Pollack JR, Perou CM, Alizadeh AA, Eisen MB, Pergamenschikov A, Williams CF, et al. Genome-wide analysis of DNA copy-number changes using cDNA microarrays. *Nat Genet* 1999;**23**(1):41−6 Available from: https://doi.org/10.1038/12640.
12. Lueking A, Horn M, Eickhoff H, Bussow K, Lehrach H, Walter G. Protein microarrays for gene expression and antibody screening. *Anal Biochem* 1999;**270**(1):103−11. Available from: https://doi.org/10.1006/abio.1999.4063.
13. Michael KL, Taylor LC, Schultz SL, Walt DR. Randomly ordered addressable high-density optical sensor arrays. *Anal Chem* 1998;**70**(7):1242−8.
14. Kuhn K, Baker SC, Chudin E, Lieu MH, Oeser S, Bennett H, et al. A novel, high-performance random array platform for quantitative gene expression profiling. *Genome Res* 2004;**14**(11):2347−56. Available from: https://doi.org/10.1101/gr.2739104.
15. DeRisi J, Penland L, Brown PO, Bittner ML, Meltzer PS, Ray M, et al. Use of a cDNA microarray to analyse gene expression patterns in human cancer. *Nat Genet* 1996;**14**(4):457−60. Available from: https://doi.org/10.1038/ng1296-457.
16. Bubendorf L, Kolmer M, Kononen J, Koivisto P, Mousses S, Chen Y, et al. Hormone therapy failure in human prostate cancer: analysis by complementary DNA and tissue microarrays. *J Natl Cancer Inst* 1999;**91**(20):1758−64.
17. Moch H, Schraml P, Bubendorf L, Mirlacher M, Kononen J, Gasser T, et al. High-throughput tissue microarray analysis to evaluate genes uncovered by cDNA microarray screening in renal cell carcinoma. *Am J Pathol* 1999;**154**(4):981−6. Available from: https://doi.org/10.1016/S0002-9440(10)65349-7.

18. Perou CM, Jeffrey SS, van de Rijn M, Rees CA, Eisen MB, Ross DT, et al. Distinctive gene expression patterns in human mammary epithelial cells and breast cancers. *Proc Natl Acad Sci USA* 1999;**96**(16):9212−17.
19. Sgroi DC, Teng S, Robinson G, LeVangie R, Hudson Jr JR, et al. In vivo gene expression profile analysis of human breast cancer progression. *Cancer Res* 1999;**59** (22):5656−61.
20. Mir KU. The hypothesis is there is no hypothesis. The Microarray Meeting, Scottsdale, Arizona, USA, 22−25 September 1999. *Trends Genet* 2000;**16**(2):63−4.
21. Debouck C, Goodfellow PN. DNA microarrays in drug discovery and development. *Nat Genet* 1999;**21**(1 Suppl.):48−50. Available from: https://doi.org/10.1038/4475.
22. Gray JW, Collins C. Genome changes and gene expression in human solid tumors. *Carcinogenesis* 2000;**21**(3):443−52.
23. Golub TR, Slonim DK, Tamayo P, Huard C, Gaasenbeek M, Mesirov JP, et al. Molecular classification of cancer: class discovery and class prediction by gene expression monitoring. *Science* 1999;**286**(5439):531−7.
24. Perou CM, Sorlie T, Eisen MB, van de Rijn M, Jeffrey SS, Rees CA, et al. Molecular portraits of human breast tumours. *Nature* 2000;**406**(6797):747−52. Available from: https://doi.org/10.1038/35021093.
25. Sorlie T, Perou CM, Tibshirani R, Aas T, Geisler S, Johnsen H, et al. Gene expression patterns of breast carcinomas distinguish tumor subclasses with clinical implications. *Proc Natl Acad Sci USA* 2001;**98**(19):10869−74. Available from: https://doi.org/10.1073/pnas.191367098.
26. Cancer Genome Atlas Research Network. Comprehensive genomic characterization defines human glioblastoma genes and core pathways. *Nature* 2008;**455**(7216):1061−8. Available from: https://doi.org/10.1038/nature07385.
27. International Cancer Genome Consortium. International network of cancer genome projects. *Nature* 2010;**464**(7291):993−8. Available from: https://doi.org/10.1038/nature08987.
28. Jaffe S. Planning for US Precision Medicine Initiative underway. *Lancet* 2015;**385** (9986):2448−9. Available from: https://doi.org/10.1016/S0140-6736(15)61124-2.
29. Ashley EA. The precision medicine initiative: a new national effort. *JAMA* 2015;**313** (21):2119−20. Available from: https://doi.org/10.1001/jama.2015.3595.

Further Reading

Blumencranz P, Whitworth PW, Deck K, Rosenberg A, Reintgen D, Beitsch P, et al. Scientific Impact Recognition Award. Sentinel node staging for breast cancer: intraoperative molecular pathology overcomes conventional histologic sampling errors. *Am J Surg* 2007;**194**(4):426−32. Available from: https://doi.org/10.1016/j.amjsurg.2007.07.008.
Pillai R, Deeter R, Rigl CT, Nystrom JS, Miller MH, Buturovic L, et al. Validation and reproducibility of a microarray-based gene expression test for tumor identification in formalin-fixed, paraffin-embedded specimens. *J Mol Diagn* 2011;**13**(1):48−56. Available from: https://doi.org/10.1016/j.jmoldx.2010.11.001.
Handorf CR, Kulkarni A, Grenert JP, Weiss LM, Rogers WM, Kim OS, et al. A multicenter study directly comparing the diagnostic accuracy of gene expression profiling and immunohistochemistry for primary site identification in metastatic tumors. *Am J Surg Pathol* 2013;**37**(7):1067−75. Available from: https://doi.org/10.1097/PAS.0b013e31828309c4.
Nystrom SJ, Hornberger JC, Varadhachary GR, Hornberger RJ, Gutierrez HR, Henner DW, et al. Clinical utility of gene-expression profiling for tumor-site origin in patients with metastatic or poorly differentiated cancer: impact on diagnosis, treatment, and survival. *Oncotarget* 2012;**3**(6):620−8.

Lo SS, Mumby PB, Norton J, Rychlik K, Smerage J, Kash J, et al. Prospective multicenter study of the impact of the 21-gene recurrence score assay on medical oncologist and patient adjuvant breast cancer treatment selection. *J Clin Oncol* 2010;**28**(10):1671−6. Available from: https://doi.org/10.1200/JCO.2008.20.2119.

Mamounas EP, Tang G, Fisher B, Paik S, Shak S, Costantino JP, et al. Association between the 21-gene recurrence score assay and risk of locoregional recurrence in node-negative, estrogen receptor-positive breast cancer: results from NSABP B-14 and NSABP B-20. *J Clin Oncol* 2010;**28**(10):1677−83 Available from: https://doi.org/10.1200/JCO.2009.23.7610.

Ahern TP, Hankinson SE. Re: Use of archived specimens in evaluation of prognostic and predictive biomarkers. *J Natl Cancer Inst* 2011;**103**(20):1558−9. Available from: https://doi.org/10.1093/jnci/djr327 author reply1559−1560.

Knezevic D, Goddard AD, Natraj N, Cherbavaz DB, Clark-Langone KM, Snable J, et al. Analytical validation of the Oncotype DX prostate cancer assay − a clinical RT-PCR assay optimized for prostate needle biopsies. *BMC Genomics* 2013;**14**:690. Available from: https://doi.org/10.1186/1471-2164-14-690.

You YN, Rustin RB, Sullivan JD. Oncotype DX colon cancer assay for prediction of recurrence risk in patients with stage II and III colon cancer: a review of the evidence. *Surg Oncol* 2015;**24**(2):61−6. Available from: https://doi.org/10.1016/j.suronc.2015.02.001.

Nguyen B, Cusumano PG, Deck K, Kerlin D, Garcia AA, Barone JL, et al. Comparison of molecular subtyping with BluePrint, MammaPrint, and TargetPrint to local clinical subtyping in breast cancer patients. *Ann Surg Oncol* 2012;**19**(10):3257−63. Available from: https://doi.org/10.1245/s10434-012-2561-6.

Cusumano PG, Generali D, Ciruelos E, Manso L, Ghanem I, Lifrange E, et al. European inter-institutional impact study of MammaPrint. *Breast* 2014;**23**(4):423−8. Available from: https://doi.org/10.1016/j.breast.2014.02.011.

Exner R, Bago-Horvath Z, Bartsch R, Mittlboeck M, Retel VP, Fitzal F, et al. The multigene signature MammaPrint impacts on multidisciplinary team decisions in ER + , HER2 − early breast cancer. *Br J Cancer* 2014;**111**(5):837−42. Available from: https://doi.org/10.1038/bjc.2014.339.

Maak M, Simon I, Nitsche U, Roepman P, Snel M, Glas AM, et al. Independent validation of a prognostic genomic signature (ColoPrint) for patients with stage II colon cancer. *Ann Surg* 2013;**257**(6):1053−8. Available from: https://doi.org/10.1097/SLA.0b013e31827c1180.

Dowsett M, Sestak I, Lopez-Knowles E, Sidhu K, Dunbier AK, Cowens JW, et al. Comparison of PAM50 risk of recurrence score with oncotype DX and IHC4 for predicting risk of distant recurrence after endocrine therapy. *J Clin Oncol* 2013;**31**(22):2783−90. Available from: https://doi.org/10.1200/JCO.2012.46.1558.

Gnant M, Filipits M, Greil R, Stoeger H, Rudas M, Bago-Horvath Z, et al. Predicting distant recurrence in receptor-positive breast cancer patients with limited clinico-pathological risk: using the PAM50 risk of recurrence score in 1478 postmenopausal patients of the ABCSG-8 trial treated with adjuvant endocrine therapy alone. *Ann Oncol* 2014;**25**(2):339−45. Available from: https://doi.org/10.1093/annonc/mdt494.

Martin M, Gonzalez-Rivera M, Morales S, de la Haba-Rodriguez J, Gonzalez-Cortijo L, Manso L, et al. Prospective study of the impact of the Prosigna assay on adjuvant clinical decision-making in unselected patients with estrogen receptor positive, human epidermal growth factor receptor negative, node negative early-stage breast cancer. *Curr Med Res Opin* 2015;**31**(6):1129−37. Available from: https://doi.org/10.1185/03007995.2015.1037730.

Prat A, Galvan P, Jimenez B, Buckingham W, Jeiranian HA, Schaper C, et al. Prediction of response to neoadjuvant chemotherapy using core needle biopsy samples with the Prosigna assay. *Clin Cancer Res.* 2015;**22**(3):560−6. Available from: https://doi.org/10.1158/1078-0432.CCR-15-0630.

Phillips KA, Van Bebber S, Issa AM. Diagnostics and biomarker development: priming the pipeline. *Nat Rev Drug Discov* 2006;**5**(6):463−9. Available from: https://doi.org/10.1038/nrd2033.

Molecular Medicine in Action

Molecular medicine includes reviews issues like the genetic basis of disease, but "molecular" does not only mean DNA. The diagnostic role of genetic processes is clear, but major benefits in health and disease are also provided by other molecules: Enzymes, antibiotics, hormones, metals, carbohydrates, lipids, and vitamins, synthetic organic and inorganic polymers. Furthermore "Medicine" involves a vital societal element; molecular intervention raises controversial ethical, legal, and financial issues.

This chapter serves as the repository of standard operating procedures (SOPs) used for molecular medicine techniques and research.

GROSSING PROCEDURES

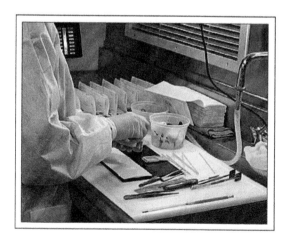

1.0 Principle/Indications

The following procedure highlights techniques and procedures used when grossing surgical pathology specimens.

2.0 Specimen Requirement/Types

Biopsy

3.0 Supplies/Equipment/Reagents

- Supplies
  - Cassettes
  - Biopsy bags
  - Sponges
  - Tweezers
  - Forceps
  - Paper towels or other absorbent paper
  - Specimen labels
  - Disposable knives
  - Decalcifier
  - Cotton swabs
- Equipment
  - Cassette microwriter
  - Hood
- Reagents
  - 10% buffered formalin, store at room temperature
  - Decal fixative (formalin based), store at room temperature
  - Ink, store at room temperature

4.0 Instrumentation

Not applicable.

5.0 Calibration

Not applicable.

6.0 Quality Control

Not applicable.

7.0 Environmental Requirements

- All grossing procedures are performed in a vented space. A hood is located in the grossing area providing ventilation.
- Observe universal precautions when handling all specimens. Wear a lab coat, gloves, and eye protection.

8.0 Operating Procedure

- Specimen Identification
  - As soon as a specimen arrives with its requisition form to the pathology laboratory, the first step to be performed, whether by a pathologist or a grosser, is to make sure that the specimen is properly identified and that all necessary information has been included on the requisition form. All primary specimen containers must be labeled with a minimum of two unique identifiers at the time of receipt. Examples of identifiers include but are not limited to: Patient full name, date of birth, requisition #, patient ID. Specimens not accompanied by two unique patient identifiers will either be returned to the client or require a signed attestation form from the physician.
  - The requisition form must include the following information:
    - Full patient name
    - Date of birth
    - Sex
    - Submitting physician's name (or designated professional personnel)
    - Source of specimen
    - Collection date
    - Clinical information, where appropriate
  - In the event one or more of required elements on the requisition is missing or needs to be verified, the physician's office will be contacted for resolution. In some instances (e.g., missing sex, collection date, or physician's name on requisition), the specimen may be processed before the missing information is obtained. In other instances (e.g., missing source, patient name, or date of birth), the specimen is accessioned, but held until the missing information is obtained or clarified before processing. The correct information is documented either on a log, the requisition form, and/or in the laboratory information system. The name of the person providing the correct information is also documented.
  - In general, it is advisable to keep a specimen in the same container throughout the gross procedure, until the time that it is discarded. If it is to be placed into another container, the specimen label

should he transferred. Putting several specimens from different patients, whether the specimens are identified with individual tags or not, into the same container is a dangerous practice and should be avoided.

- Each specimen is assigned a unique surgical pathology case number (a unique identifier assigned by the laboratory from a preprinted ribbon). The assigned number will be affixed to the requisition as well as on the specimen container (not the lid but on the body of container) at the time of grossing.
- Tissues from multiple designated sites can be submitted on one requisition slip. Multiple part specimens are designated with alphabetical letters. Examples of acceptable specimen labeling as to source are as follows:
  - Requisition states sites as 1. ECC, 2. 5:00, 3. 6:00.
    Specimen containers labeled ECC, 5:00, 6:00.
    Specimen containers labeled 1,2,3.
    These would be labeled (surgical #) A, B, C, respectively.
- If specimen containers are not designated as to source, and the submitting clinician cannot be reached for clarification, this must be stated in the gross description. Alphabetical designations will be assigned and special attention is given to any distinguishing gross features that might enable identification of the source.
- Preparation for Grossing
  - Line up specimens and requisitions in numerical order. Make sure the assigned number is placed on the body of the specimen container itself.
  - Avoid grossing similar specimens consecutively. For example, interspace products of conception (POC) specimens or endometrial currettings with other types of tissue. This can be best accomplished in the accessioning phase by assigning nonconsecutive surgical numbers for similar types of specimens. The purpose for this is to prevent cross contamination or mix-up either at the grossing bench or during histology processing.
  - Organize necessary tools, blades, cassettes, biopsy bags, and biopsy sponges so they are readily accessible.
  - Grossing is performed on a nonporous cutting board, covered by paper towels, in a vented space.
- Grossing
  - Fixation principles
    - The proper fixation of a piece of tissue depends on its size and nature. Small solid specimens (not exceeding 2 cm in their smallest dimension) can be fixed properly when placed in a container with a sufficient amount of fixative (10 times or more the volume of the tissue). Cystic specimens with a thin wall will

also be well fixed, even when they are of a somewhat larger size. Since specimens received in the laboratory are collected the previous day, more than enough time has passed to properly fix these specimens by the time they are received. The vast majority of biopsy specimens received at clinical labs will be of this category.

- For larger and/or more solid specimens, additional fixation time may be required. Additionally, if a specimen is received where the formalin to specimen ratio is clearly insufficient, additional fixation time may be required. Typically, if additional time is required, it is fixed one additional day.

• Handling and cutting the specimen

- Gentleness should be used throughout the gross procedure if one is to avoid producing disturbing artifacts. Tissues are fragile and should be handled with care. Forceps without teeth should be used for picking up small specimens from containers and transferring them to cassettes, with special care taken to avoid putting any undue pressure on the tissue. Forceps with teeth are better suited for holding a portion of the specimen that is not going to be sampled for histology while another portion is being cut with a scalpel.

- Mucosal surfaces are particularly susceptible to trauma. The temptation to rub one's fingers over them should be resisted with determination. Similarly, prolonged washing of mucosal membranes with tap water is discouraged. A strong jet of water will detach mucosal cells, and the water itself will lead to the swelling and rupturing of the superficial cells when it is left in contact with them long enough. A gentle and brief washing with formalin is highly preferable.

- Specimens are also susceptible to drying artifacts, especially before fixation. The time during which the tissue is left in contact with the air, outside of a fixative solution, should be reduced to a minimum. Good preparation for grossing minimizes this.

- The act of cutting a specimen in two halves or in a series of slabs is not as simple as it may seem, if it is to be done properly. The selection of the right plane of section is important and entirely dependent of the structures present. In general, the cut should be planned in such a way as to obtain the maximum information regarding the relationship between the lesion and the normal anatomic structures. The cut should be carried out with a smooth, continuous motion of the hand, rather than in a seesaw fashion, in order to avoid making unnecessary marks. Whenever ridges or irregularities are present on the surface of a specimen, it is recommended that the cuts be made perpendicular to them.

- Decalcification
  - Tissues containing calcium salts need to be decalcified
    thoroughly. The decision whether or not a specimen requires
    decalcification can be made at the time of gross examination, but
    is usually performed by a histotechnologist after the specimen is
    processed using a decalcifying instrument, which combines heat
    and rotation to speed up the process.
  - Tissues should be thoroughly fixed in formalin or other fixatives
    before being submitted for decalcification. The fluid used for
    this purpose is a formalin-based decalcification solution. Blocks
    are transferred into a beaker of the solution and placed on a
    decalcifying instrument for a few hours. Following
    decalcification, the tissues are washed thoroughly in water and
    processed as usual.
- Sampling
  - It is important that all the material submitted to the laboratory
    be grossly examined and properly sampled. This is particularly
    true for small punch or needle biopsies, in which only one of the
    fragments (sometimes the smaller one) may contain the
    diagnostic area. If gauze or other extraneous material has been
    immersed in fixative, all of its sides need to be examined for
    small fragments of tissue attached to it. The underside of the
    container's lid should also be inspected.
  - The most important dimension to remember for the purposes of
    processing is their thickness. This should never exceed 4 mm,
    and, ideally, it should be between 2 and 3 mm. The more
    uniform the thickness throughout the sample, the better the
    impregnation and the easier the orientation in the paraffin block
    will be. The other two dimensions are important only to the
    extent that they should not exceed those of the cassette being
    used. The sample should be somewhat smaller than the cassette
    so that it can move freely once it is placed inside, or infiltration
    is likely to be compromised. This also applies to specimens
    submitted in numerous small fragments, such as those obtained
    from endometrial curettings. It is important to avoid packing the
    cassette with the fragments if adequate infiltration is to be
    achieved.
  - Cross contamination of specimens can be avoided by thoroughly
    cleaning the instruments and the cutting board between cases
    and avoiding placing specimens in cassettes that are so small or
    fragmented that they could pass through the cassette holes while
    being shaken in the tissue processor. Place biopsy sponges in the
    cassettes, on either side of the specimen, or wrap the specimens
    in a biopsy bag before putting them in the cassette. Care should

be exercised so that the tissues are not squeezed during the procedure. Thoroughly wet the biopsy bags or sponges with formalin fixative before administering the specimen.

- Orientation of the samples
  - The orientation of the sample in the paraffin block to be performed by the histology technician also needs to be considered at the time of gross examination. One should remember that the technician has not seen the sample in relation to the whole specimen, and is working with tissue that by then has been infiltrated in hot paraffin. For all these reasons, it is imperative that the specimens are cut and prepared in such a way that the technician will have no difficulty orienting them properly. For many specimens, this is inconsequential. For example, fragments obtained from an endometrial curetting can be oriented at random. But for other specimens, orientation is very important. One surface may exhibit a feature not present on the other side, or it may be smoother and more homogeneous. The use of biopsy sponges aids in keeping the specimens oriented in the same manner during tissue processing.
  - Specimens having a lining of some sort, whether it is cutaneous, mucosal, or a surgical margin, need to be oriented in such a way that the lining can be clearly seen in the section. In order to achieve this, a cut has to be made perpendicular to that surface and the sample has to be mounted "on edge" by the technician. If the sample is large enough and the sections have been well made, an experienced technician should have no trouble orienting them correctly. If there is any doubt, consult a pathologist.
- Surgical margins
  - It is important to know whether a tumor or another lesion is close to or exceeds surgical margins. Inking the surgical margins allows a pathologist to make this determination microscopically. Ink is used undiluted and applied to the tissue with a cotton swab. In order to prevent diffusion of the ink, it is recommended that the tissue be blotted with gauze before the ink is applied and that the ink is allowed to dry about 30 seconds before the specimen is cut or placed in fixative. At the time of sectioning by the grosser, the painted margin should be placed against the cutting board so that it will be the last part of the specimen to be cut. In this way, penetration of the ink into the specimen by the cutting knife can be prevented.

- Protocol for submission of specific specimen types
  - General biopsy [includes gynecological (GYN), gastrointestinal (GI), prostate, anorectal, etc.]

    Submit entirely. For endometrial biopsies, submit tan-colored tissue in one block, and blood clots in a separate block, if possible.
  - Cervical biopsy—SpiraBrush

    Remove the SpiraBrush CX brush head from the vial and while holding the brush head over the biopsy bag, straighten the brush head with forceps or tweezers.

    Place the brush head firmly on the biopsy bag. With a blade or smooth forceps, scrape the entire surface area of the brush head onto the biopsy bag by turning the brush head as needed to scrape the entire surface area of the brush head onto the biopsy bag.

    Pour the entire remaining contents of the vial through the biopsy bag and submit entirely.

    Add a drop of Eosin (optional), fold biopsy bag, place in cassette, and process the sample as for regular biopsies.
  - Cervical cone/Loop Electrosurgical Excision Procedure (LEEP) specimens

    Leave for a pathologist before proceeding (must be performed with direct supervision). Submit entirely after inking the rough surface. If stitch is present, designate this as 12.00 pm Cut the cone into quadrants with proper orientation of the mucosal surface. Label cassettes according to clock position (e.g., Cassette #1, 12.00—3.00 pm, #2, 3—6, #3, 6—9, #4, 10—12).
  - Large colonic polyps

    Leave for a pathologist before proceeding (must be performed with direct supervision) colonic polyps that are 1 cm or larger. Ink base of stalk if visible, and section serially with proper orientation if possible. Submit entirely.
  - POC

    Search for villi and submit one block. If not sure if villi are sampled, submit three blocks and wait for further instruction from a pathologist. Do not submit the entire specimen, unless it will be three blocks in toto. If the specimen is submitted fresh, check first if a chromosomal analysis or culture is requested on the requisition. Do not pour formalin into the specimen right away.
  - Skin

    Await instruction from a pathologist. Send outs for dermatopathology include punch biopsies, clinical impression of rash, dermatitis, atypical nevus, or suspected melanomas.

- Intrauterine device (IUD)

    Scrape any tissue from the device with a scalpel and submit entirely.

    If the specimen is submitted fresh, check first if a culture is requested on the requisition. Do not pour formalin into the specimen right away.

- Others (e.g., small breast lumpectomy specimen)

    Other specimen types may be received not listed in this procedure. If this were to occur, the grosser will ask the pathologist for instructions.

- Direct vs indirect pathologist supervision of grosser
    - Types of specimens that nonpathologist personnel can gross with indirect pathologist supervision are small specimens that are entirely submitted and those small specimens that can be sectioned without any knowledge of anatomy. They are as follows:

        POC

        Small biopsies from various sources

        Endometrial and endocervical curettings

        Polyps (cervical and small GI polyps less than 1 cm)

        Small tumor removal (lipoma, condyloma, nevus)

        IUD removal and simple foreign body identification

    - Types of specimens that nonpathologist personnel can gross with direct pathologist supervision are as follows:

        Cervical cone resections with stitch orientation, large LEEP specimens

        Colonic polyps larger than 1 cm

        Resections for tumor (skin, breast lumpectomy, etc.)

        Unusual specimens

    - Note: Specimens that require dissection are grossed by nonpathologist personnel under direct pathologist supervision. The said personnel meet specific qualifications required under CLIA regulations (see document discussed later). All specimens grossed requiring direct pathologist supervision are documented on the "Grossing Supervision by Pathologist" sheet discussed later.

- Specimen remnants after sampling
    - Specimen remnants should be saved in formalin for a specified length of time in such a fashion so that they are easily retrievable and recognizable. The rules previously stated for the identification of the container apply here as well.
    - The specimen should never be discarded until the case has been signed out and kept for a minimum of two weeks after sign-out.

  - Place all specimen containers for the day, containing remnant or not, into a dated clear plastic bag. Store the bag in the gray metal cabinet in the histology laboratory.
- Gross description
  - The gross description of each case is accomplished through written documentation on the "Grossing Log Sheet" discussed later. The following steps apply:
    Write the patient name and date.
    Write the surgical case number.
    Write the number of containers received per requisition.
    Write the specimen part letter and source (e.g., A, labeled ECC).
    Note: It is essential that the patient's name, surgical number, part letter, and source be compared between the requisition and the container for every specimen. This will act as a check for labeling errors or specimen part mix-ups.
  - A description of the specimen and processing is then documented. This includes:
    Mention of the nature of the fixative (e.g., received in formalin, in alcohol, unfixed).
    Description of the specimen: Number, color, type, measurements (discussed later).
    Description of the sectioning process, including whether special techniques are used (e.g., inking), and whether representative sections or the entire specimen is submitted. Tissue cassette number and block designation is given. If more than one block is submitted from a specimen, each block is designated by a number. If a cassette represents an identifiable landmark, a key to sections is provided (e.g., if cassette A1 corresponds to the clock portion of a cervical cone specimen, this is indicated).
    If only one specimen is submitted for microscopic examination, no further identification (in the way of letters) is necessary. If two or more specimens are submitted, these should be properly labeled with letters. The letters to be used and the order followed are those of the English alphabet, rather than the initial of the specimen or some other code.
  - Initial and date the bottom of each grossing log sheet, staple to each corresponding requisition, and forward to the transcriptionists. Transcriptionists will enter gross description information into the laboratory information system, and well as any relevant clinical information provided on the requisition.
  - Fill out the "Histology Daily Worksheet" discussed later. Grossers are responsible for filling out the case #, # sections,

type of tissue, and grosser initial columns. Forward this sheet to the embedding center.
- Cassette microwriter
- Blocks are then labeled by the cassette microwriter before being sent into the tissue processor.
- Tissue processing
- Place blocks into the automated tissue processor.
- Accessioning
  - After all specimens are grossed and submitted for further processing, the cases are accessioned into the laboratory information system.
  - Grossers will enter patient demographics, a unique accession number, a unique surgical pathology case number, and the specimen source into the system. Labels are then generated containing the case number, accession number, patient name, and date of receipt. These generated labels are placed on the requisition and on the body of each specimen container.

9.0 Maintenance

Not applicable.

10.0 Calculations

Not applicable.

11.0 Result Reporting

See operating procedure discussed earlier.

12.0 Procedural Notes

Specimens received fresh, in saline or other nonformalin type fluid should be checked with the client if, in fact, a biopsy is what the client actually is requesting. Do not add formalin to the biopsy container until the biopsy order is verified. Clients sometimes will order a biopsy on a sample by mistake and instead want a culture or chromosome analysis on a specimen.

13.0 Limitations

Not applicable.

14.0 Instrumentation Downtime

Not applicable.

15.0 References

Not applicable.

Grossing Log Sheet

Case Number_____ Patient Name_____

Date_____
Number of Containers_____

Label on Container 1_____Label on Container 2_____

Label on Container 3, 4, etc._____

Container 1:
# of Tissue Samples_____ Size of Samples (range or aggregate)_____

Nature of Fixative_____Color of Tissue_____Grossly Evident Lesion: NO_____ YES_____

Other Gross Description (eg. Fetal Parts, Bloody, Mucus)_____
Submitted (circle one)   in toto;   Representative Sections
Number of Cassettes (circle one)   one, two, three, four, five, other
Circle if Applicable: inked;   Margins Submitted in Separate Cassette

---

Container 2:
# of Tissue Samples_____ Size of Samples (range or aggregate)_____

Nature of Fixative_____Color of Tissue_____Grossly Evident Lesion: NO_____ YES_____

Other Gross Description (eg. Fetal Parts, Bloody, Mucus)_____
Submitted (circle one)   in toto;   Representative Sections
Number of Cassettes (circle one)   one, two, three, four, five, other
Circle if Applicable: inked;   Margins Submitted in Separate Cassette

---

Container 3:
# of Tissue Samples_____ Size of Samples (range or aggregate)_____

Nature of Fixative_____Color of Tissue_____Grossly Evident Lesion: NO_____ YES_____

Other Gross Description (eg. Fetal Parts, Bloody, Mucus)_____
Submitted (circle one)   in toto;   Representative Sections
Number of Cassettes (circle one)   one, two, three, four, five, other
Circle if Applicable: inked;   Margins Submitted in Separate Cassette

---

Use Another Sheet if Needed	**Key:**	
	Fixatives:	F = formalin U = unfixed A = alcohol S = saline
	Descriptions:	SAF = soft and friable STF = soft tissue fragment
		SPT = soft polypoid tissue SAS = soft and spongy
		WB = with brush NB = no brush
	Colors:	B = brown T = tan W = white Y = yellow P = pigmented

Grosser Initials_____Date_____

SPECIMEN ADEQUACY

1.0 Principle/Indications

The Bethesda System 2001 recommendations include a specimen adequacy component be present on GYN cytopathology reports. The Bethesda System 2010 recommendations for thyroid fine needle aspiration (FNA) reporting also include a specimen adequacy component be present on non-GYN cytopathology reports. The following is a description of these recommendations.

2.0 Specimen Requirement/Types

- GYN cytology
- Non-GYN cytology

3.0 Supplies/Equipment/Reagents

- Supplies: N/A
- Equipment: N/A
- Reagents: N/A

4.0 Instrumentation

Not applicable.

5.0 Calibration

Not applicable.

6.0 Quality Control

Not applicable.

7.0 Environmental Requirements

Not applicable.

8.0 Operating Procedure

- GYN cytology
  - Specimens are diagnosed as either satisfactory or unsatisfactory for evaluation, as are indicated with the following.

- Satisfactory for evaluation (describe presence or absence of endocervical transformation zone component and any other quality indicators, e.g., partially obscuring blood, inflammation, etc.)

  If the patient has a hysterectomy or a vaginal smear is submitted, the specimen is considered satisfactory for evaluation without a description, provided enough squamous cells are present on the smear (discussed later for requirements). The presence of glandular cells is noted and submitted to QC or a pathologist for confirmation.

  If the patient has a supracervical hysterectomy, the presence or absence of endocervical transformation component is noted on the cytology report.

  Professional judgment may be needed when applying numerical criteria in certain cases (e.g., atrophy).

- Unsatisfactory for evaluation:

  Specimen processed and examined, but unsatisfactory for evaluation (specify reason).

  Too few squamous cells

  Poor preservation

  Totally obscured by blood

  Totally obscured by white blood cells

- Note: If abnormal cells are noted on the smear, the specimen is never considered unsatisfactory. An interpretation is given, and a description of adequacy is noted on the report.
- ThinPrep adequacy requirements for satisfactory assessment
  - A total of 5000 well-preserved epithelial cells must be present for a smear to be considered satisfactory. Each of the following criteria refers to well visualized and preserved cells in each corresponding field of view.

    10X objective and FN20 ocular: 50 cells per field

    40X objective and FN20 ocular: 3.1 cells per field

    10X objective and FN22 ocular: 60.5 cells per field

    40X objective and FN22 ocular: 3.8 cells per field
- SurePath adequacy requirements for satisfactory assessment
  - A total of 5000 well-preserved epithelial cells must be present for a smear to be considered satisfactory. Each of the following criteria refers to well visualized and preserved cells in each corresponding field of view:

    10X objective and FN20 ocular: 118.3 cells per field

    40X objective and FN20 ocular: 7.4 cells per field

    10X objective and FN22 ocular: 143.2 cells per field

    40X objective and FN22 ocular: 9.0 cells per field

- Conventional adequacy requirements for satisfactory assessment
  - A total of 8,000–12,000 well-preserved epithelial cells must be present for a smear to be considered satisfactory. This must be estimated using judgment. The following can be used as a guide. At least 10% of the smear must be covered with well-preserved epithelial cells for a conventional pap slide to be considered satisfactory.
- Non-GYN cytology
  - Adequacy requirements for thyroid FNAs
    - A minimum of six groups of benign follicular cells, each containing at least 10 cells, are required to be considered satisfactory for evaluation (and benign). There are exceptions to this rule:

      Solid nodules with cytologic atypia: Specimens are considered satisfactory for evaluation by definition, and do not require a minimum number of follicular cells.

      Solid nodules with inflammation: patients with lymphocytic (Hashimoto's) thyroiditis, thyroid abscesses, or granulomatous thyroiditis may contain numerous inflammatory cells and do not require a minimum number of follicular cells.

      Colloid nodules: specimens containing thick, abundant colloid are considered satisfactory for evaluation if the colloid predominates the slide/smear.
  - Anal-rectal ThinPrep specimens
    - The same requirements as for GYN cytology specimens submitted via ThinPrep apply to anal-rectal specimens received in ThinPrep vials, the exception being that glandular cells are substituted for endocervical cells.
  - Sputum specimens
    - Macrophages must be present for a sputum specimen to be considered satisfactory for evaluation.
  - Other non-GYN cytology sites
    - Self-judgment is used by cytotechnologists and pathologists in assessing adequacy of other specimen sites.

9.0 Maintenance

Not applicable.

10.0 Calculations

Not applicable.

11.0 Result Reporting

Not applicable.

12.0 Procedural Notes

Not applicable.

13.0 Limitations

Not applicable.

14.0 Instrumentation Downtime

Not applicable.

15.0 References

- The Bethesda System 2001
- The Bethesda System for Reporting Thyroid Cytopathology, 2010.

SPECIMEN COLLECTION INSTRUCTIONS

1.0 Principle/Indications

This policy provides specimen collection instructions for specimens routinely submitted for anatomic pathology testing.

2.0 Specimen Requirement/Types

- GYN cytology
  - Cervical, endocervical, and/or vaginal specimens (Fig. 4.1)
- Non-GYN cytology
  - Urine
  - Rectal
  - Sputum
  - Tzanck smear
  - Breast discharge
  - FNA
    - Various sites, e.g., thyroid, breast, head and neck, prostate, etc.
  - Fluids
    - Various sites, e.g., pleural, peritoneal, synovial, etc.
  - Other miscellaneous (Fig. 4.2)

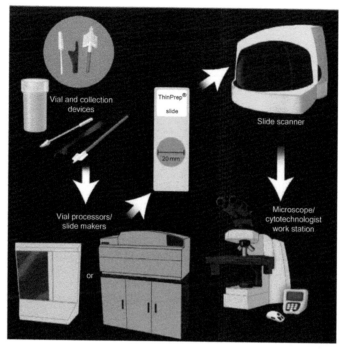

FIGURE 4.1 Cytopreparation, instrumentation, and automated screening in gynecologic cytology.

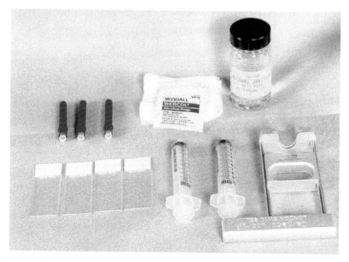

FIGURE 4.2 Fine needle aspirate preparatory tools (syringe holder, plastic syringe) (10cc disposable plastic syringe), disposable needles, 22-gauge, 1 inch and 1.5 inches long with clear plastic hubs, glass slides, and fixative.

- Biopsy
  - GYN
  - GI
  - Anal rectal
  - Prostate
  - POC
  - Skin
  - Oral cavity
  - IUD
  - Polyps
  - Foreign body
  - Other miscellaneous

3.0 Supplies/Equipment/Reagents

Clients will routinely submit the following to the laboratory for anatomic pathology testing:

- Conventional slides for GYN cytology (spray-fixed) or non-GYN cytology (spray-fixed and/or air dried)
- ThinPrep containers for GYN or non-GYN cytology
- SurePath containers for GYN cytology
- Sterile containers (fixed and/or unfixed) for non-GYN cytology
- Prefilled 10% buffered formalin containers for biopsy

For GYN pap test collection, the following are examples of supplies and reagents that are routinely used:

- Speculum
- Gauze
- Cotton-tipped swabs
- Saline
- Biohazard specimen bags
- Requisition form
- Collection device (one or more of the following)
  - Spatula
  - Cervical brush
  - Brush/spatula combination device
  - Broom
  - Cytobrush
  - Cytobroom
- Transport medium
  - Glass slides (if submitting conventional pap test)
  - Spray-fixative or alcohol (for conventional slides)
  - Plastic or cardboard slide holders (for conventional slides)

- ThinPrep container (for ThinPrep test)
- SurePath container (for SurePath test)

For non-GYN test collection, the following are examples of supplies and reagents that are routinely used, depending on the specimen site and type of specimen being submitted:

- Biohazard specimen bags
- Requisition form
- Collection device (various)
- Transport medium
  - Glass slides (if submitting conventional slides)
  - Spray-fixative
  - Saccomanno fixative
  - Cytolyt fixative
  - Alcohol fixative
  - Sterile containers

For biopsy test collection, the following are examples of supplies and reagents that are routinely used, depending on the specimen site and type of specimen being submitted:

- Biohazard specimen bags
- Requisition form
- Collection device (various)
- Transport medium
  - Prefilled 10% buffered formalin containers
  - Sterile containers

All specimens should be considered infectious. Observe universal precautions when handling specimens from all patients. Follow all manufacturer's instructions related to any reagents used for specimen collection, and do not use any past their expiration dates.

4.0 Instrumentation

Not applicable.

5.0 Calibration

Not applicable.

6.0 Quality Control

Not applicable.

7.0 Environmental Requirements

All reagents and specimen containers collected for anatomic pathology testing should be stored at room temperature, unless manufacturer's instruction says otherwise. There are some exceptions to this, although rare. An example is if any fluid for cytology is collected unfixed and delivery of the specimen to the laboratory will be delayed. It is best to refrigerate to preserve specimen integrity.

Specimen	Optimal specimen collection schedule	Volume	Specimen handling instructions
Cerebrospinal fluid (CSF)	Within 7 days of onset	1–2 mL	
Amniotic fluid		3 mL	
Vitreous fluid (eye)		1 mL	
Urine	Within 2 weeks of onset	5 mL	
Blood		5–7 mL	In yellow ACD tube
Bone marrow aspirate		2–5 mL	In yellow ACD tube
Bronchoalveolar lavage (BAL)		3–5 mL	
Swabs (nasal, throat, nasopharyngeal, vesicle/lesion, rectal, eye/conjunctive, genital)	NP: Within 5 days VESCL/GEN swabs—as early as possible	Swab in M4	In viral transplant media M4
Aspirates (nasal, tracheal, sinus, vesicle)		1–2 mL	
Nasal wash	Within 5 days of onset	3–5 mL	
Feces	Within 2 weeks of onset	5 mL	In container without preservatives
Tissue		Variable	In sterile saline or viral transport media

8.0 Operating Procedure

- GYN specimen collection
  - Position of the patient

- Sample collection is usually performed with the patient in the lithotomy position (please see figure discussed later).

Lithotomy

- ෴ Patient lies in supine position with buttocks at the lower break of the table.
- ෴ The legs are flexed in the
- ෴ hip (90 degrees) and
- ෴ abducted (30 degrees)
- ෴ in the hip.

- ෴ The knees are bent 70 to 90 degrees.
- ෴ The lower legs are supported on padded leg shells.

- Preparation of the cervix
  - Once the patient is positioned, a sterile single-use disposable bivalve speculum of appropriate size should be gently inserted into the vagina, avoiding direct pressure in the sensitive anterior structures (e.g., urethra). Water may be used to lubricate and warm the speculum. Use of lubricating jelly is discouraged. If it must be used, use sparingly and one that does not contain carbomers. Excess jelly may interfere with ThinPrep sample processing. Several sizes of specula should be available so that an appropriate device may be chosen for the patient. Very young patients, patients with little sexual experience, and elderly patients with vaginal atrophy, require the use of a smaller, narrower speculum than women who are sexually active. The speculum must be positioned so that the entire face of the cervix appears at the end of the instrument since a sample from this area is necessary for adequate specimen collection. A large, cotton-tipped swab is often useful for helping to position the cervix.
  - It is important to obtain a sample that is not obscured by blood, mucus, or inflammatory exudates. Following correct positioning of the speculum in the vagina, if there is excess mucus or other discharge present, it should be gently removed with ringed forceps using a folded gauze pad. Inflammatory exudates may be removed by placing a dry 2 × 2-inch (5.08 × 5.08 cm) piece of

gauze over the cervix and peeling it away as it absorbs the exudate. The cervix should not be cleaned by washing with saline as it may result in an inadequate specimen sample. The sample should also be obtained before the application of acetic acid.

- Visual inspection of the lower genital tract and cervix through the speculum is a prerequisite to optimal sample collection. Squamous epithelium of the ectocervix has a smooth, pearly opaque appearance. Native columnar epithelium of the endocervix is slightly reddish with a "cobblestone" surface. The transformation zone (where native endocervical columnar epithelium has undergone conversion to "immature" metaplastic squamous epithelium) has an intermediate, variegated appearance. This is the area that is most important to sample as most abnormalities generate in the transformation zone.

- Conventional pap test collection using spatula and cervical brush
  - Observe universal precautions for collecting and handling all specimens.
  - Label the frosted end of the glass slide with the patient's name before sample collection. Insert speculum, which may be slightly moistened with water or saline if necessary. Do not use lubricating jelly unless absolutely necessary.
  - Visually inspect the cervix for abnormalities. Identify the transformation zone, if visible, and direct sampling efforts to encompass this area. If an elevated, ulcerated, necrotic, or exudate-covered lesion is observed, arrangements should be made for biopsy following cytology sampling.
  - Choose the contoured end of the spatula that best conforms to the anatomy of the cervix and the location of the transformation zone. Rotate the spatula at least 360 degrees about the circumference of the cervical os and ectocervix, while maintaining firm contact with the epithelial surface.
  - Do not smear the sample at this time unless the specimen is to be immediately fixed. Hold the spatula between the fingers of the nonsampling hand (or rest it on the glass slide) with the specimen face-up, while the cervical brush material is collected without delay.
  - Insert the cervical brush into the os. Some bristles should still be visible. This will minimize inadvertent sampling of the lower uterine segment. With gentle pressure, rotate the brush, only 90 to 180 degrees to minimize bleeding.

Note: Brushes have circumferential, radiating bristles that come in contact with the entire surface of the os upon insertion. This is in contrast to the edge of the spatula, which is in contact with only a fraction of the epithelial surface at any time. Therefore, the brush need only be rotated one quarter turn (90 degrees) while the spatula must be rotated at least one full turn (360 degrees).

- The use of both the spatula and cervical brush is recommended for optimal sampling. The preferred order of spatula and brush sampling has not been subjected to large-scale studies. However, obtaining the spatula specimen first diminishes the possibility of blood contamination due to trauma by the brush. Although performing the brush collection first may increase the yield of exfoliated abnormal cells by the spatula. One option is to sample the ectocervix twice, both before and after obtaining the endocervical brush specimen.
- Spread the material collected on the spatula and cervical brush evenly over the glass slide by twirling the handles.

    Note: The object is to quickly but evenly spread the cellular material in a layer on the glass slide. Thin out large clumps of material as much as possible, while avoiding manipulation, which can damage cells. To avoid the development of air-drying artifact, transfer the material from both sampling instruments to the slide within a few seconds and fix immediately with spray-fixative.

- The following are three smearing options for transferring the material to the glass slide.

    Smear the spatula sample across the slide; roll the brush material directly over the previously spread sample. Immediately fix the slide. However, with this method the ability to localize the origin of the cells may be lost.

    Smear the spatula sample over the left-hand side of the slide, cover the right side with cardboard, and immediately spray-fix. Roll the brush material onto the right side of the slide and immediately spray-fix.

    Collect, transfer, and immediately fix each sample separately using two different slides.

- Whichever smearing option is chosen, immediately fix the specimen on the slide(s) by either immersing the slide in 95% ethanol or coating the slide with a surface spray-fixative. If using spray-fixation, hold the container 12 inches (30.5 cm) from the slide to avoid disrupting the cells. Spray-fixed or

liquid-coated slides must be allowed to dry completely before packaging for transport.
  - Place slides in either a plastic or cardboard slide holder and place in biohazard bag. Submit to the laboratory with properly filled out requisition form.
- Other collection instruments used for conventional pap testing
  - Observe universal precautions for collecting and handling all specimens.
  - Another collection instrument is a plastic "broom-like" brush that simultaneously samples the endocervix and ectocervix. To use the "broom," the long central bristles are inserted into the os until the lateral bristles bend against the ectocervix and are rotated a total of three to five times in a clockwise or counter-clockwise direction. To transfer material, both sides of the "broom" are stroked once across the slide. Immediately spray-fix and submit to the laboratory, as indicated earlier.
  - Although not recommended, the cotton swab (saline-moistened) is another collection instrument that may be used. However, use of a cotton-tipped applicator usually provides less cellular samples. To transfer material, firmly press the cotton swab against the slide, rotate, and smear several times lengthwise across the slide. Immediately spray-fix and submit to the laboratory, as indicated earlier.
- ThinPrep Pap test collection using brush/spatula combination device
  - Observe universal precautions for collecting and handling all specimens.
  - Label the ThinPrep vial with the patient's name and a second unique identifier, such as the date of birth.
  - Sample ectocervix with a plastic spatula, as indicated in conventional pap test collection earlier.
  - Rinse spatula in the ThinPrep vial's PreservCyt fluid by swirling vigorously 10 times. Place cap on vial and discard collection device.
  - Sample endocervix with an endocervical brush, as indicated in conventional pap test collection earlier.
  - Rinse the brush in the ThinPrep vial's PreservCyt fluid by rotating the device in the solution 10 times while pushing against the side of the ThinPrep vial wall. Swirl the brush vigorously to further release material. Discard the collection device.

- Firmly tighten the ThinPrep vial cap, place in biohazard bag, and submit to the laboratory with properly filled out requisition form.
- ThinPrep Pap test collection using broom
  - Observe universal precautions for collecting and handling all specimens.
  - Label the ThinPrep vial with the patient's name and a second unique identifier, such as the date of birth.
  - Obtain a sample from the cervix using the broom-like device, as indicated in conventional pap test collection earlier.
  - Rinse the collection device in the ThinPrep vial's PreservCyt fluid by pushing the brush into the bottom on the vial 10 times, forcing the bristles to bend apart to release the cervical material. As a final step, twirl the brush between the thumb and forefinger vigorously to further release cellular material. Discard the collection device.
  - Firmly tighten the ThinPrep vial cap, place in biohazard bag, and submit to the laboratory with properly filled out requisition form.
- SurePath pap test collection using cytobrush or cytobroom
  - Observe universal precautions for collecting and handling all specimens.
  - Label the SurePath vial with the patient's name and a second unique identifier, such as the date of birth.
  - Obtain a sample from the cervix using the cytobrush or cytobroom, which are similar to the cervical brush and broom used in ThinPrep collection.
  - Break off the tip of the cytobrush or cytobroom, and place in the SurePath vial containing preservative fluid.
  - Firmly tighten the SurePath vial cap, place in biohazard bag, and submit to the laboratory with properly filled out requisition form.
- Samples submitted for hormonal evaluation (maturation index)
  - Samples for hormonal evaluation should be obtained using a spatula to gently scrape the epithelium from the upper third lateral vaginal wall. The source of the specimen should be vaginal, and relevant patient history should be provided.
- Requisition requirements for GYN pap tests
  - Requisitions sent to the laboratory must be completely filled out with the following information:
    Full patient name
    Date of birth

Sex

Source of specimen

Last menstrual period (LMP)

Patient history/clinical information

Test name

- Non-GYN specimen collection
  - Specimens collected for non-GYN cytology testing can be from a variety of sources.
  - Observe universal precautions for collecting and handling all specimens.
  - Label the transport vial(s) with the patient's name and a second unique identifier, such as the date of birth. If conventional slides are submitted, label with a patient's name.
  - Urine

    Collect urine for cytology in a sterile container and add either Cytolyt, Saccomanno fluid, or alcohol. A 50–50 mix of specimen to fixative should be submitted if possible. If no fixative is available, the specimen may be sent unfixed, although this is not encouraged as cells will degenerate over time and may cause difficulty in diagnosis.

    Urine specimens may be voided, catheterized, or from a bladder washing. Be sure to indicate the collection method on the requisition.

    If the urine needs other testing in addition to cytology, such as a culture, it is best to split the urine specimen at the office into two containers and send them with separate requisitions. If this is not possible, one urine container may be submitted and the laboratory will split the specimen. However, the urine must be sent unfixed. This is not encouraged due to possible cell degeneration.

    Place in biohazard bag, and submit to the laboratory with properly filled out requisition form.
  - Rectal

    After collecting the specimen, swirl the tip of the collection device into a ThinPrep vial's PreservCyt fluid multiple times. Press the tip into the side of the container to further release cellular material.

    Be sure to indicate the source of the specimen as "rectal" on the requisition.

    Place in biohazard bag, and submit to the laboratory with properly filled out requisition form.

- Sputum

  Submit sputum specimens in a sterial container containing either Cytolyt, Saccomanno fluid, or alchohol. If no fixative is available, the specimen may be sent unfixed, although this is not encouraged as cells will degenerate over time and may cause difficulty in diagnosis.

  Be sure to indicate the source of the specimen as "sputum" on the requisition.

  Place in biohazard bag, and submit to the laboratory with properly filled out requisition form.

- Tzanck smear

  After collecting the specimen, smear the collection device tip onto a properly labeled slide as you would with a conventional pap test collection (see discussed earlier).

  Immediately fix the specimen with a spray-fixative.

  Be sure to indicate that the specimen is a Tzanck smear and from what source of the body it came from. The laboratory will look for herpes related changes and indicate whether or not they were seen on the report.

  Place slides in either a plastic or cardboard slide holder and place in biohazard bag. Submit to the laboratory with properly filled out requisition form.

- Breast discharge

  Breast discharge, or nipple discharge specimens may be submitted as conventional slides or as fluid in a sterile container. If sending conventional slides, immediately fix the specimen with a spray-fixative. If sending in as fluid, add either Cytolyt, Saccomanno fluid, or alcohol. A 50−50 mix of specimen to fixative should be submitted if possible. If no fixative is available, the specimen may be sent unfixed, although this is not encouraged as cells will degenerate over time and may cause difficulty in diagnosis.

  Place specimen in a biohazard bag and submit to the laboratory with a properly filled out requisition form. If sending conventional slides, place in either a plastic or cardboard slide holder.

- FNA

  FNAs can come from a variety of body sites. For all body sites, submit four conventional slides if possible, two immediately spray-fixed and two air dried. If fluid is left over in the syringe, submit in a sterile container, and add either Cytolyt, Saccomanno fluid, or alcohol, in a 50−50 mix of specimen to fixative, if possible.

It is especially important to provide the body site of the specimen and relevant clinical information on the requisition when submitting FNAs for non-GYN cytology. For example, if sending in a thyroid FNA, the size of the lesion, whether cold or cot, cystic or solid, etc. is important information to give the laboratory.

Place specimen in a biohazard bag and submit to the laboratory with a properly filled out requisition form. If sending conventional slides, place in either a plastic or cardboard slide holder.

- Fluids

  Fluids can come from a variety of body sites. Submit fluids in a sterile container, and add either Cytolyt, Saccomanno fluid, or alcohol, in a 50–50 mix of specimen to fixative, if possible.

  Provide the body site of the fluid being submitted for non-GYN cytology on the requisition (e.g., peritoneal, pleural, synovial, etc.), and any relevant clinical information.

- Requisition requirement for non-GYN tests
  - Requisitions sent to the laboratory must be completely filled out with the following information:

    Full patient name

    Date of birth

    Sex

    Source of specimen

    Patient history/clinical information

    Test name

- Biopsy specimen collection
  - Specimens collected for biopsy testing can be from a variety of sources.
  - Observe universal precautions for collecting and handling all specimens.
  - Label the transport vial(s) with the patient's name, a second unique identifier, such as the date of birth, and the specimen source for each container submitted. Submit all tissue in prefilled 10% buffered formalin containers, unless otherwise specified.
  - GYN

    Cervical

    SpiraBrush cervical

    Endocervical (curettage and/or biopsy)

    Endometrial (curettage and/or biopsy)

Cones

LEEP

Vulva

POC

If only a biopsy is requested, send in formalin.

If a biopsy and chromosome analysis is requested, split the specimen at the office and submit the biopsy in formalin and the chromosome analysis in a sterile container fresh or with saline added. Specimens with requests for chromosomal analysis are sent out to a reference lab.

- GI

Esophagus

Duodenum

Stomach

Small intestine

Large intestine

- Anal rectal
- Prostate
- IUD

If only a biopsy is requested, send in formalin.

If a biopsy and culture is requested, send in fresh. The sample will be sent to microbiology for culture first. Formalin will then be added and any tissue adhered to the IUD will be scraped off and tested.

- Polyps (various sources)
- Skin
- Oral cavity
- Foreign body
- Requisition requirement for biopsy tests
  - Requisitions sent to the laboratory must be completely filled out with the following information:

Full patient name

Date of birth

Sex

Source of specimen(s)

Patient history/clinical information

Test name

9.0 Maintenance

Not applicable.

10.0 Calculations

Not applicable.

11.0 Result Reporting

Not applicable.

12.0 Procedural Notes

Not applicable.

13.0 Limitations

Specimens received without proper identification may result in reporting delays as clarification will be requested from clients through phone calls or other verification means. Requisitions for testing that are not fully complete may also cause delays pending verification or the request of additional information.

14.0 Instrumentation Downtime

Not applicable.

15.0 References

- http://www.thinprep.com/hcp/specimen_collection.html
- http://www.bd.com/tripath/physicians/surepath.asp
- http://www.cytopathology.org/website/article.asp?id=384

IMMUNOHISTOCHEMISTRY AND HPV IN SITU PROCEDURES

1.0 Principle/Indications

Immunohistochemical (IHC) techniques allow for the visualization of specific cellular antigens in tissues. Specimen slides are pretreated, then incubated with primary antibodies from rabbit, mouse or other species, followed by incubation with a linking reagent (secondary antibody), labeling reagent (tertiary antibody) and finally, with a chromogenic substrate system (i.e., 3,3'-diaminobenzidine (DAB), 3-amino-9-ethylcarbazole (AEC), etc.). The net result is the development of a distinct brown or red reaction product at the site of the target antigen in the tissue.

2.0 Specimen Requirement/Types

Biopsy

3.0 Supplies/Equipment/Reagents

- Supplies
  - Microscope "plus" slides with sections cut at approximately 4–5 μm
  - Covertiles
  - Pipette tips
  - Staining dishes
  - Coverslips
  - Bond mixing stations
  - Bond cleaning kit
  - Bond open containers
  - Titration container inserts
  - Slide labels and ribbons
- Equipment
  - Pipettes
  - Oven
- Reagents
  - DAB refine detection kit, store refrigerated at 2–8°C
  - Bond dewax solution, store between 2 and 26°C
  - Bond epitope retrieval solution 1, store refrigerated at 2–8°C
  - Bond epitope retrieval solution 2, store refrigerated at 2–8°C
  - Bond wash solution, store refrigerated at 2–8°C
  - Bond antibody diluent, store refrigerated at 2–8°C
  - Distilled water
  - Bond enzyme pretreatment kit, store refrigerated at 2–8°C
  - 95% alcohol, store at room temperature
  - 100% alcohol, store at room temperature
  - Xylene, store at room temperature
  - Mounting media, store at room temperature
  - Vimentin antibody, store refrigerated at 2–8°C
  - CD138 antibody, store refrigerated at 2–8°C
  - Helicobacter pylori antibody, store refrigerated at 2–8°C
  - P16 antibody, store refrigerated at 2–8°C
  - KI-67 antibody, store refrigerated at 2–8°C

4.0 Instrumentation

- Leica Bond 3 Stainer, S#3210924
- Leica Bondmax Stainer S#M210646

5.0 Calibration

- Bond 3 and Bondmax Stainer
  - The initial and periodic calibrations on the stainers are performed by the vendor's service personnel. Records are kept in the pathology department.
- Pipettes
  - Calibrations are performed yearly by specific vendors. Records are kept in the QA coordinator's office.

6.0 Quality Control

- Quality control is essential for accurate, reproducible, and reliable IHC staining results.
- Commercially available antibodies should not be assumed to be monospecific or immunoreactive. They must be evaluated according to specification data and instructions.
- Reagents
  - Store reagents according to manufacturer's instructions. If the reagent is reconstituted, indicate on the bottle label the content, concentration if applicable, storage properties, date prepared and the expiration date applicable.
  - Do not use expired reagents/antibodies. Infrequently used antibodies can be frozen in aliquots. Do not refreeze the aliquots, discard after use.
  - Always validate the results with the appropriate positive control that shows the expected staining result. If the control is weak or negative, check the antibody expiration date and repeat.
  - Allow frozen or refrigerated reagents to reach room temperature before use.
  - Change all xylene and alcohol solutions weekly or as appropriate.
  - Check the wash buffer pH at the time of reconstitution, monitor the pH periodically, and document Change buffer if pH is out of range.
- Antibodies
  - Use a matched set of unexpired antibodies and reagents.
  - Optimally dilute antibodies to give reproducible staining results. Each new concentrated or prediluted antibody must be evaluated to determine the optimal working dilution, incubation time, retrieval solution type, etc.
  - All antibodies are stored according to the manufacturer's antibody storage information.
  - Pretreat or antigen retrieve slides as needed, according to manufacturer's recommendation; include variations in length of incubation time or in the type of retrieval solution/enzyme.

- To obtain optimal dilution, first follow the suggested dilution from the antibody supplier. Set-up the following gradations of dilutions according to the recommended range. Start with half-fold below the suggested low range, the low range, the high range and twice the high range as needed.

For example: Suggested dilution = 1:100−1:200

- 1:50
- 1:100
- 1:200
- 1:400
  - For negative controls, evaluate negative internal control tissue and/or negative control block selected by the pathologist. Record the results of the evaluation during review with the pathologist.
  - After the initial evaluation, detection kits and antibodies from a different lot or from a different vendor need to be reevaluated in parallel with the old lot (using tissue from different blocks/cases) starting with the optimal antibody dilution in current use. If the reactivity is optimal, use the same conditions. If weak or too strong, reevaluate. If the new antibody is from the same lot, it does not need to be reevaluated as long as the positive control remains optimally stained.
- Positive and negative controls
  - Select appropriate positive control tissue to be used for the surgical case.
  - For each antibody being performed, place patient section on the precut positive control slide so that they are to be run together. Positive controls can be shared between cases if run in parallel.
  - For each patient tissue block, run a negative control slide using a nonimmune serum from same species as the primary antibody or the diluent/buffer in place of the primary antibody. Use the same staining protocol as the primary antibody. If different pretreatment is required for each of the primary antibodies within a case, the negative control protocol will follow the harshest pretreatment (high pH is more aggressive than pH 6).
  - Verify that the positive control section stains positive and the negative control section stains negative. This is verified by the pathologist and documented.
  - In cases where there is no positive control (control section fell off), internal controls (i.e., staining of expected positive cells or staining of normal tissue elements which are supposed to be reactive) are acceptable.

- Should the positive and/or negative controls fail to stain appropriately, check the concentrations and expiration dates of all reagents and look for any system failures. Correct the source of failure and repeat the run.
- Record the reactivity of each control block in a log and the date when the block is tested.
- Other information
  - For each surgical block, cut the number of blanks that equal the number of antibodies or probes being tested times 2, plus one blank for the negative control.
  - Use only calibrated equipment.
  - Staining with monoclonal antibody V9 vimentin is useful when problems occur due to overfixation. Because of its ubiquitous presence in blood vessels and stromal cells, positive vimentin staining is a reliable indicator of tissue integrity. This antibody is used when performing lot-to-lot verification on DAB refine kits.

7.0 Environmental Requirements

- Wear appropriate personal protective equipment when handling slides and reagents.
- A hood is required when xylene is in use, and when coverslipping slides with mounting media.

8.0 Operating Procedure

- Specimen requirements
  - Tissues must be adequately fixed and processed as for paraffin blocks. The standard fixative is 10% neutral buffered formalin (10% NBF, commercially available).
  - The tissue must be fixed for at least 6 hours, preferably not longer than 24 hours, at room temperature. Optimal tissue size to fixative ratio is $10 \times 10 \times 5$ mm in 100 mL of 10% NBF).
  - Decalcification of tissues requires 30–60 min in commercially available decal solution, followed by additional fixation.
- Specimen handling
  - Paraffin sections are cut at 4–5 μm thick and placed on properly identified positively charged slides. Excess water is tapped off, and then they are placed in a 58–60°C oven for 20–30 min (or longer if not ready to stain). Control slides are stored at 2–8°C in the properly identified box. The first control slide cut from the same block is identified with the block designation.

- Specimen accessioning
  - This procedure is used to ensure tracking of specimens that require IHC studies.
  - Upon receipt of the IHC request form (discussed later) from the pathologist, the case is assigned an IM #, and the block is retrieved from histology for sectioning.
  - Blank slides are identified by the Surg path # (including specific block # if any) and the IM #. The number of slides to be prepared per case is the number of antibodies requested X 2, allowing a slide for the Neg control as well as extra slides for any repeats or additional antibodies or in situ testing.
  - Sections from the patient block are placed on precut control slides when appropriate. Positive controls can be shared by different cases and this is cross-referenced on the slide label. Certain antibodies do not require a positive control section because internal control tissue can be identified in the patient tissue.
  - Slide labels are prepared before the time of staining on either of the Bond stainers. Each label includes the following:
    - Case # w/block/IM#
    - Patient name
    - Ab name
      w/ Pos (+/S or Q, case #,omit yr) (+/Int)
  - Follow the step-by-step IHC staining procedure for paraffin embedded tissue. Decalcified tissue is stained the same way as nondecalcified paraffin sections. Staining is performed at room temperature on the Bond 3 and/or Bondmax stainer.
- Preliminary checks:
  - Before starting the Bond 3 and/or Bondmax systems, do the following periodically:
    - Check generally for cleanliness.
    - Check the aspirating probe tubing for blockages or bubbles. If you see bubbles, prime the system by turning the processing module off, and then on again.
    - Wipe the aspirating probe with 70% alcohol, being careful not to bend the aspirating probe (this is best done after a run).
    - Wipe the heater blocks with 70% alcohol.
    - Check that the slide staining assembly springs are intact. Replace them if necessary.
    - Make sure the bulk waste and hazardous waste containers are not full or near full.
    - Make sure the slide tray is clean.
    - Check that the bulk reagent containers are full or near full.

- Check that the slide labeler has an adequate supply of labels. If the roll looks depleted, then ensure that a replacement roll is available.
- Start the Bond 3 and/or Bondmax system
  - If everything is determined to be in order, start the system(s).
  - If the processing module(s) and computer are not on, turn them on now.
  - When the computer is running, start the Bond software.
  - Select the appropriate instrument tab that you will be using.
  - Once the software has started, check the status screens to ensure there are no processing module errors. Correct any errors before attempting to run any batches.
  - Power up the slide labeler.
  - Check the protocols
    - Select the protocols icon from the function bar.
    - Select the protocol in the table, click "Open," and note the preferred detection system in the "Edit protocol properties" dialog ("Bond Polymer Refine Detection," or "Bond Polymer Refine Red Detection").
    - Make sure that the protocol is selected as "Preferred."
  - Check the reagents
    - This check assumes that you have stock of the required antibodies and detection kit, and that these have been registered in the reagent inventory section of the software.
    - Select the reagents icon from the function bar.
    - On the Setup tab, select "Primary" and "All" with the "Show" radio buttons at the bottom of the screen. Locate each of the antibodies that you need in the list and ensure that it is checked as "Preferred." If not, select the antibody and click "Open" to open the "Edit Reagent Properties" dialog. Click the "Preferred" radio button at the bottom of the dialog and then click "Save."
    - Now go to the "Inventory" tab and select "Reagents," "In stock" and "Preferred" with the "Show" radio buttons at the bottom of the screen. All the antibodies you need should appear with the volumes available. Make sure that there is sufficient volume for each antibody (in general, about 150 μL per slide)
    - On the same tab, select "Detection Systems" with the "Show" radio button and check that the preferred detection system is listed in the table, and that there is enough volume.
    - Ensure that the ambient temperature is between 18 and 26°C to meet all staining performance requirements.

- Setting up slides
  - Click the Slide setup screen icon from the function bar.
  - Click "Add Case" at the slide setup screen.
  - Click in the "Case ID" field and type the surg path # with specific block if any.
  - Click in the "Patient name" field and type the name in the format "last name, first initial."
  - Leave other fields blank.
- Entering slide details
  - Click "Add Slide" to display the add slide dialog.
  - Ensure "Test Tissue" is selected as the tissue type (if necessary, click the "Test Tissue" radio button to select it).
  - Select a dispense volume suitable for the tissue size (use 150 μL unless otherwise specified by a pathologist).
  - Click the "IHC" radio button to specify the process.
  - Click in the "Marker" field to display a list of primary antibodies.
  - Select the antibody from the list. The software automatically enters the default protocol for the antibody in the "Staining Protocol" field.
  - Click in the "Preparation" field and select the preparation to be used for the slide. The preparation may be either "Dewax" or "Bake and Dewax."
  - To add epitope retrieval steps, click in either the "HIER Protocol" or "Enzyme Protocol" field and select the one required from the dropdown list. Click "Close" to close the "Add Slide" dialog.
  - In the comment field, type in the "w/cont" or " + /S0000" or " +/int), then click "Add Slide." The slide is then added to the slide list. The "Add Slide" dialog remains open.
  - Repeat steps to add additional slides to be run. One can choose "Copy Case" so that details don't have to be reentered.
  - After all slides have been selected, review the details in the slide list.
  - If you need to change details for a slide, right-click on the slide, select "Slide Properties" from the submenu, change the details as required, and then click "OK."
  - The next case can now be added as described earlier, if running a different antibody.
  - Print slide labels and place them on the slides.
  - You can use "Panels" to quickly add a number of slides that you commonly use. For an explanation of panels and how to create

and use them, see the "Reagent Panels Screen" section of the Bond manual.

- You can add control slides to control cases by selecting either "Negative Tissue" or "Positive Tissue" instead of "Test Tissue" during the "Entering Slide Details" steps. Set-up control reagents by selecting the appropriate reagent from the marker list during slide setup.

- Editing a case
  - If you edit details of a case for which slide labels have been printed, you will have to print the labels again before you can run the slides.
  - To edit the details of a case, select it in the list and then click "Edit Case." The software displays the "Case Properties" dialog. You can use this in the same way as the "Add Case" dialog described previously.

- Creating new cases and/or slides after imaging
  - Using the default system settings, follow the procedure discussed later to add case and slide information after slides have been loaded and imaged.
  - Load slides onto the processing module in the usual manner. There is no need to create cases or slides in the Bond software or print labels; hand written or third party labels can be used.
  - The system will not recognize the slides. It will display images of the labels.
  - To launch the assisted ID dialog do one of the following:
       Double-click on the slide image.
       Right-click on the image and select "Select manually" from the submenu.
  - The active slide is highlighted on the slide tray. The dialog includes an enlarged image of the label to assist with slide identification.
  - Hold the cursor over the slide in the right-hand pane to see an even greater enlargement of the label.
  - The left-hand pane lists all cases with current slides and empty cases that have not yet expired. Resurrected cases (see the "Case Duplication and Resurrection" section of the Bond manual) with no slides configured for them also appear, by default (see the "Setting New Case and New Slide Options" section of the Bond manual).
  - The center pane shows any slides that have been configured for the case that is currently selected in the left-hand pane, and that have not yet been matched with any slides imaged on the processing module.

- To create a new case, click "New Case."
- You can now create a new case for the selected slide in the normal manner.
- Once created, the new case is automatically selected in the case list.
- To create a new slide for the case you just created, click "New Slide". Note that this button becomes active when a case is selected. This opens the "Add Slide" dialog.
- Create a new slide in the software for the physical slide selected in the right-hand pane, in the normal manner (refer to the "Creating a Slide" section of the Bond manual). When it is added, the new slide is displayed in the center pane of the dialog (i.e., while the new case remains selected in the left-hand case list).
- Ensuring that the correct label image is still selected in the right-hand pane, press "Insert" to match it with the new slide in the center pane. The slide is removed from the center pane and the label image in the right-hand pane is replaced to show the system information for the slide, as it was entered for the new slide you have just created. If you match slides incorrectly, you can undo this step by selecting the slide in the right-hand pane and slicking "Remove".
- The slide can now be processed in the usual manner. Repeat the procedure of creating new cases and slides for remaining slides in the slide tray.
- Creating new protocols
  - You can create new protocols by copying existing protocols. When you copy a protocol, the type of protocol remains fixed and cannot be altered later. Thus if you wish to create a new IHC protocol you must copy an existing IHC protocol; for an HIER protocol, copy an existing HIER protocol and so on.
  - To copy a protocol, select it from the list in the "Protocol Setup" screen. Then click the "Copy" button. A copy of the selected protocol will now appear in the "New Protocol Properties" dialog ready for editing.
  - To save the new protocol, click "Save" from the "Edit Protocol Properties" dialog.
  - If you do not wish to save the new protocol, click "Cancel" at any time.
- Registering Bond reagents and detection systems
  - Registering a reagent adds a new package of reagent to the inventory. The reagent must be listed in the "Reagent Setup" screen before you can register a package of it. You must register reagent packages before using them on the Bond 3 or Bondmax.

- To register a Bond reagent package, scan the ID on the side of the container. The software will display the "Add Reagent Package" dialog.
- To register a Bond detection system, scan both IDs on the side of the reagent tray carrying the detection system containers.
- Registering non-Bond reagents
  - You must add the details of the reagent to the Bond system from the "Reagent Setup Screen" before you can register physical amounts of it.
  - You must use non-Bond reagents with a Bond Open Reagent Container, and you must register that container as for Bond reagent containers. When you read an open container ID, the "Add Reagent Package" dialog opens with the "Reagent Name" field blank. You must select a name from the dropdown list, and fill in other fields as necessary (you must enter an expiration date), then click "OK."
- Manual ID entry of reagents
  - In some cases, IDs on reagent packages may become damaged to the point where the Bond system cannot read them. If the Bond system fails to read a reagent ID, do the following from the "Reagent Inventory Screen."
  - Click "Enter ID." The Bond software displays the "Manual ID Entry" dialog.
  - Enter the package number in the top row. The package number is alongside the ID on reagent packages, and above the ID on detection systems.
  - If there is more than one ID (e.g., detection system), then click "Validate" after entering each ID. The software will check the ID. If it is valid, it will display the details of the package.
  - Click "Close" when you have finished entering and checking the details.
- Reagent inventory screen
  - The inventory screen allows one to register reagents and detection systems, as well as change the details and minimum stock volumes of individual reagents registered. To display this screen, go to the "Reagent Setup" screen, then click the "Inventory" tab. The "Volume" field shows the total amount of the reagent that the Bond software calculates is available. The "MinStock" field shows the minimum stock volume. Reagents that have less than the minimum stock volume are highlighted in red.
  - When displaying detection systems, the table displays "Name", "Catalog No", "Vol" and "MinStock" columns. The radio

buttons at the bottom of the table in the "Reagent Inventory" screen determine what is displayed in the table.

- Select "Reagents" to show only reagents registered in the system, or "Detection Systems" to show only detection systems registered in the system.
- Note that when viewing detection systems the other "Show" options are disabled and all detection systems are automatically displayed in the list.
- Select "In Stock" to show only reagents for which there are volumes recorded, "Low" to show reagents that require reordering, or "All" to show all reagents registered with the Bond system, whether or not stock is held. These options do not affect detection system visibility.

• Slide history
- To see slide history details or to generate run events, batch, case, or service reports, select the "History" icon from the function bar. The "Slide" tab that shows the slide history is active by default. Otherwise, click to make it active.
- The "Slide History" screen has a calendar function on the right of the screen. You can use this function to specify the reporting period. Only the details of the slides processed within this period are displayed.
- When the slide history screen is first opened, the "Time Period to Show" dropdown list is set to "Day." The present date appears in both the "From" and "To" fields. The dates are displayed in the short date format. Dates are entered in the fields using a combination of the "Previous" and "Next" buttons in the "Time Period to Show" dropdown list. You cannot enter information into the "To" or "From" fields.

• Titration kit
- The titration kit is used to optimize the concentration of primary antibodies. Small volumes of each primary antibody concentration can be prepared and placed into the titration inserts (test tubes). Each container may be used for a total of 40 mL of reagent. There is a dead volume of 200 μL for the insert.
- Titration of concentrated antibodies can be achieved using serial twofold dilutions:
    Label three inserts with appropriate dilutions for each antibody or probe.
    Make a starting dilution in the first insert of 700 μL.
    Dispense 350 μL of Bond Primary Antibody Diluent into insert 2 and 3.

From the starting dilution, transfer 350 μL to insert 2 and gently mix.

From insert 2, transfer 350 μL to insert 3 and gently mix.

- Delayed start (overnight run)
  - Prepare slides as for regular run, except during the selection of the "Slide Properties" step. Click on "Bake and Dewax" to get to the drop down list, and then click the 10 hours delay.
  - To change the number of hours of delay, go to "Configuration" on the toolbar.
  - After selecting the delay mode, continue as usual. When the start button is clicked, verify that you are in the delay mode by looking for the complete run time above the Start/Stop bar. The complete time should be the next morning.
- Staining protocols
  - The following lists the steps of the protocols programmed into the Bond software for each antibody. All steps dispense 150 μL of reagent. Pretreatment steps are listed in the chart discussed later "Table of Primary Antibodies and Methods in Use."
  - See "Table of Primary Antibodies and Methods in Use" discussed later for pretreatment steps.
  - P16, Ki-67, H. pylori, and Vimentin

Step	Reagent	Incubation time
1	Primary	30 min
2	Bond Wash Solution	0
3	Bond Wash Solution	0
4	Bond Wash Solution	0
5	Postprimary	8 min
6	Bond Wash Solution	2 min
7	Bond Wash Solution	2 min
8	Bond Wash Solution	2 min
9	Polymer	8 min
10	Bond Wash Solution	0
11	Bond Wash Solution	2 min
12	Bond Wash Solution	0
13	Peroxide Block	3 min

14	Bond Wash Solution	0
15	Bond Wash Solution	0
16	Bond Wash Solution	0
17	Deionized Water	0
18	Deionized Water	0
19	Mixed DAB Refine	5 min
20	Mixed DAB Refine	5 min
21	Deionized Water	0
22	Deionized Water	0
23	Deionized Water	0
24	Hematoxylin	10 min
25	Deionized Water	0
26	Bond Wash Solution	0
27	Deionized Water	0

- CD138

Step	Reagent	Incubation time
1	Peroxide Block	5 min
2	Bond Wash Solution	0
3	Bond Wash Solution	0
4	Bond Wash Solution	0
5	Primary	15 min
6	Bond Wash Solution	0
7	Bond Wash Solution	0
8	Bond Wash Solution	0
9	Postprimary	8 min
10	Bond Wash Solution	2 min
11	Bond Wash Solution	2 min
12	Bond Wash Solution	2 min
13	Polymer	8 min

14	Bond Wash Solution	0
15	Bond Wash Solution	2 min
16	Bond Wash Solution	0
17	Mixed DAB Refine	5 min
18	Bond Wash Solution	0
19	Bond Wash Solution	0
20	Bond Wash Solution	0
21	Mixed DAB Refine	5 min
22	Deionized Water	0
23	Deionized Water	0
24	Deionized Water	0
25	Hematoxylin	10 min
26	Deionized Water	0
27	Bond Wash Solution	0
28	Deionized Water	0

9.0 Maintenance

- When operating inside the Bond processing modules (e.g., daily cleaning around the slide staining assemblies) switch the processing modules off.
- Hazardous fluids may collect in various parts of the processing modules. Use gloves and immediately clean up spills.
- Slide staining assemblies in the instruments may be very hot and cause severe burns. Do not touch the slide staining assemblies or their surrounding parts within 20 minutes of cessation of operation of a processing module.
- Clean all removable components by hand only.
- Do not clean any part with solvents, harsh or abrasive cleaning fluids, or harsh or abrasive cloths.
- Periodically check for leaks, or worn or damaged equipment. Contact manufacturer for replacement of parts.
- Soak covertiles in 100% alcohol and completely dry. Then can be reused until visually dark-brown in color.
- Refer to "Leica Bondmax and Bond 3 Cleaning and Maintenance" chart discussed later for detained maintenance protocols.

10.0 Calculations

Not applicable.

11.0 Result Reporting

- The staining results on a case are incorporated into the text of the surg path report by the pathologist, who will then correlate the findings with the hematoxylin and eosin (H&E) stain and render a final diagnosis.
- Reference range: Negative
- Interpretation
  - Positive staining with DAB refine detection will appear brown.
- Turnaround time for cases run on the Bond 3 or Bondmax is generally one additional day (Fig. 4.3).

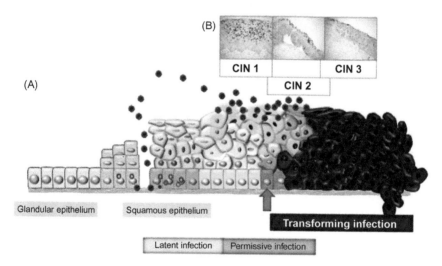

FIGURE 4.3 Correspondence of HPV E6/E7 RNA staining patterns with HPV infective biology.

(A) HPV infection of basal cells occurring via microabrasions to the cervical epithelium may give rise to latent and subsequently productive (permissive) infections. The transforming phase is associated with upregulated E6 and E7 expression blue *arrow*). (B) The data from the present study suggest HPV E6 and E7 RNA expression detected by chromogenic in situ hybridization corresponds with HPV infective mode which in turn correlates with CIN grade. [Source: Image (A) (Refs. 15 and 16) is reproduced with kind permission courtesy of Professor Magnus von Knebel Deobervitz, University of Heidelberg, Germany.]. https://doi.org/10.1371/journal.pone.0091142.g004.

- Examples
  - Positive p16 antibody staining with DAB refine detection

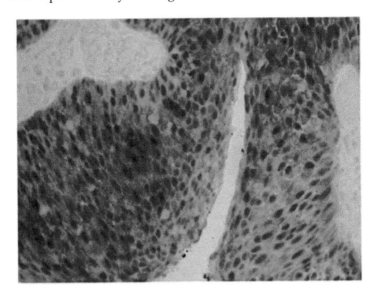

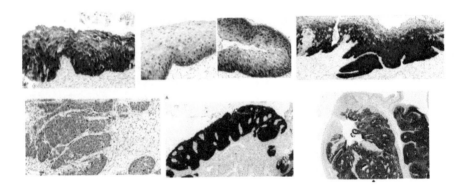

- False-positive results

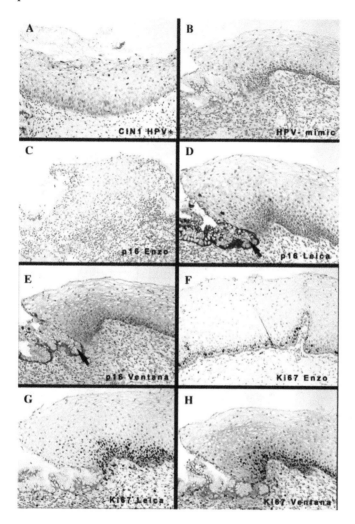

12.0 Procedural Notes

Not applicable.

13.0 Limitations

- Tissue staining is dependent on the handling and processing of the tissue prior to staining. Improper fixation, freezing, thawing, washing, drying, heating, sectioning, or contamination with other tissues or fluids may produce artifacts, antibody trapping, or false negative results.
- Inconsistent results may be due to variations in fixation and embedding methods, or to inherent irregularities within the tissue.
- Excessive or incomplete counterstaining may compromise proper interpretation of results.
- The clinical interpretation of any staining or its absence should be complemented by morphological studies using proper controls and should be evaluated within the context of the patient's clinical history and other diagnostic tests by a qualified pathologist.
- Unexpected negative reactions in poorly differentiated neoplasms may be due to loss or marked decrease of expression of antigen or loss or mutation(s) in the gene(s) coding for the antigen. Unexpected positive staining in tumors may be from expression of an antigen not usually expressed in morphologically similar normal cells, or from persistence or acquisition of an antigen in a neoplasm that develops morphologic and IHC features associated with another cell lineage (divergent differentiation). Histopathologic classification of tumors is not an exact science and some literature reports of unexpected staining may be controversial.
- Reagents may demonstrate unexpected reactions in previously untested tissues. The possibility of unexpected reactions even in tested tissue groups cannot be completely eliminated due to biological variability of antigen expression/target nucleic acid in neoplasms, or other pathological tissues.
- Normal or nonimmune sera from the same animal source as secondary antisera used in blocking steps may cause false negative or false-positive results due to autoantibodies or natural antibodies.
- False positive results may be seen due to nonimmunological binding of proteins or substrate reaction products. They may also be caused by pseudoperoxidase activity (erythrocytes), endogenous peroxidase activity (cytochrome C), or endogenous biotin (e.g., liver, breast, brain, kidney) depending on the type of immunostain used.
- False negative cases may result from various factors, including true antigen decrease, loss or structural change during tumor "dedifferentiation," or artefactual change during fixation or processing. As with any IHC test, a negative result means that the antigen was not detected, not that the antigen was absent in the tissues assayed.

14.0 Instrumentation Downtime

Two processing modules are available for use (Bond 3 and Bondmax). The Bond 3 is the primary processing module that will be used for IHC testing. The Bondmax will be used when increased work-loads warrant and/or if the Bond 3 is down.

15.0 References

Leica Bond User Manual

Leica Bond 3 Cleaning and Maintenance

Month_____   Year_____   S/N: 3210924

	1	2	3	4	5	6	7	8	9	10	11	12	13	14	15	16	17	18	19	20	21	22	23	24	25	26	27	28	29	30	31
BEFORE STARTING																															
Check Bulk and Hazardous Waste Bottles																															
Check Bulk Reagents																															
END OF RUN/DAY																															
Clean Each Slide Staining Assembly																															
Clean Covertiles																															
Clean Slide Trays																															
Wipe Outside of the Aspirating Probe with an Alcohol Wipe																															
WEEKLY																															
Clean Covers and Lid																															
Clean Lower Drip Tray																															
Top Off Bulk Reagents																															
Clean Slide Labeler																															
Shut Down Software and Turn Off Processing Module for at Least 30 Seconds																															
MONTHLY																															
Replace Mixing Stations or Clean Probe with Cleaning Kit																															
Clean Bulk Containers																															
AS NEEDED																															
Replace Aspirating Probe and Tubing																															
Change Syringe and Tip																															
Change Probe																															

Supervisor Review:

Comments/Corrective Action:

Leica Bondmax Cleaning and Maintenance

Month_____   Year_____   S/N: M210646

	1	2	3	4	5	6	7	8	9	10	11	12	13	14	15	16	17	18	19	20	21	22	23	24	25	26	27	28	29	30	31
BEFORE STARTING																															
Check Bulk and Hazardous Waste Bottles																															
Check Bulk Reagents																															
END OF RUN/DAY																															
Clean Each Slide Staining Assembly																															
Clean Covertiles																															
Clean Slide Trays																															
Wipe Outside of the Aspirating Probe with an Alcohol Wipe																															
WEEKLY																															
Clean Covers and Lid																															
Clean Lower Drip Tray																															
Top Off Bulk Reagents																															
Clean Slide Labeler																															
Shut Down Software and Turn Off Processing Module for at Least 30 Seconds																															
MONTHLY																															
Replace Mixing Stations or Clean Probe with Cleaning Kit																															
Clean Bulk Containers																															
AS NEEDED																															
Replace Aspirating Probe and Tubing																															
Change Syringe and Tip																															
Change Probe																															

Supervisor Review:

Comments/Corrective Action:

Immunohistochemistry Request Form

Specimen # /Block _____Tissue _____Pathologist_____Date_____

Patient Name _____Comments_____

_____ p16

_____ MIB-1/Ki67

_____ H. pylori _____

_____

_____

_____

_____

_____

_____

_____ CD138

Table of Primary Antibodies and Methods in Use

Antigen/ probe	Clone/ vendor	Application	Control tissue	Primary Ab/probe dilution	Pretreatment**	Storage
CD138	MI15/Leica	Plasma cells	Tonsil	Predilute	H2 × 20′	2–8°C
H. pylori	Polyclonal/ Leica	H. pylori	Infected tissue	1:200	H1 × 20′	2–8°C
Ki-67	MIB-1/ DAKO	Proliferation marker	Cervix or int. control	1:50	H1/H2 × 30′	2–8°C
P16 (CINtec)	E6H4/ CINtec	Dysplasia	Dysplastic cervix/vul/ anus	Predilute	H1 × 20′	2–8°C
Vimentin[a]	V9/Leica	Mesenchymal	Appendix	Predilute	H2 × 20′ or H1 × 10′	2–8°C

[a]Used for lot-to-lot evaluation of DAB Refine kits only.
Notes:
- **Pretreatment
- H1 = Bond heat retrieval reagent, pH 6.0 (ER1)
- H2 = Bond heat retrieval reagent, high pH (EDTA, 8.8) (ER2)
- ***In-house protocol
- Primary AB incubation of 15′
- Primary AB incubation of 30′
- The Leica bond autostainer system uses Bond polymer DAB detection with online dewax and heat retrieval capabilities.

KWIK-DIFF STAINING

1.0 Principle/Indications

The Kwik-Diff stain (please see examples in the figures discussed later) is used to stain non-GYN conventional slides received air dried. It is a manual stain (Figs. 4.4 and 4.5).

2.0 Specimen Requirement/Types

- Non-GYN cytology
  - Urine
  - Rectal
  - Sputum
  - Tzanck smear
  - Breast discharge
  - FNA
    - Various sites, e.g., thyroid, breast, head and neck, prostate, etc.
  - Fluids
    - Various sites, e.g., pleural, peritoneal, synovial, etc.
  - Other miscellaneous

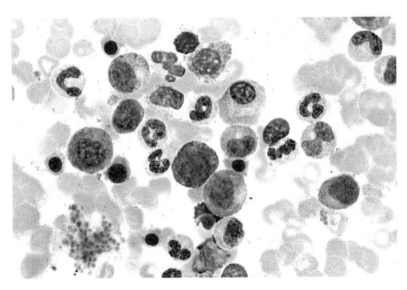

FIGURE 4.4 Shandon Kwik-Diff stains. Thermo Scientific related applications: Anatomical pathology.

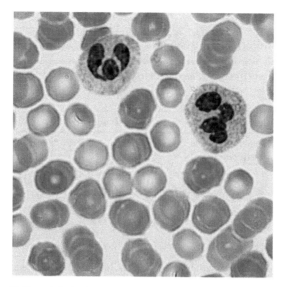

FIGURE 4.5 Differential Quik Stain Kit (Modified Giemsa) is a high quality, rapid turnaround staining kit that serves many purposes in the cost conscious laboratory environment. Differential Quik Stain Kit may be used for rapid blood smears for differential assessment, as well as detecting H. pylori microorganisms. The stain is very useful to pathologists for immediate interpretation of FNA biopsies. Kit contains a fixative for air-dried cell suspensions and/or touch preparation slides.

3.0 Supplies/Equipment/Reagents

- Supplies
  - Coplin jars
- Equipment: N/A
- Reagents
  - Kwik-Diff Solution 1 (Thermo), store at room temperature
  - Kwik-Diff Solution 2 (Thermo), store at room temperature
  - Kwik-Diff Solution 3 (Thermo), store at room temperature
  - Distilled water

4.0 Instrumentation

Not applicable.

5.0 Calibration

Not applicable.

6.0 Quality Control

- Track lot numbers on all reagents used on designated tracking charts (date opened, lot number, expiration date).
- Documented stain checks are performed each day the stain is performed.

Symptom	Cause	Remedy
Blue/black precipitate seen	Hematoxylin has precipitated	Filter hematoxylin If precipitate will not filter out (Gill's hematoxylin) change and use fresh
Floater	Stains and reagents contain dislodged cells	Change or filter solution
Halos seen	Microscope not aligned	Use Kohler illumination
	Mounting medium has incorrect refractive index	Change mounting medium
Shrunken cells	Inappropriate fixative used	Use correct fixative
Xylene is cloudy (milky)	Contaminated with water	Change xylene and absolute alcohols using clean dry dishes Change absolute alcohols more frequently
Water droplets seen	Contaminated clearing agent or mounting medium	Use fresh solutions

7.0 Environmental Requirements

- Observe universal precautions when handling all specimens. Wear a lab coat, gloves, and eye protection.
- All staining is performed under a fume hood (with the exception of the running water steps).

8.0 Operating Procedure

- Prepare three coplin jars by filling each adequately, one with Solution #1 (fixative), the second with Solution #2, and the third with Solution #3.
- Dip air-dried smears five times (1 second per dip) into Solution #1. Allow excess to drain into jar and blot edge on absorbent paper.

- Dip slide(s) five times (1 second per dip) into Solution #2. Allow excess to drain into jar and blot edge on absorbent paper.
- Dip slide(s) five times (1 second per dip) into Solution #3. Allow excess to drain into jar and blot edge on absorbent paper.
- Rinse slides by dipping in distilled water.
- Allow slides to air dry.
- Proceed to coverslipping on the Consul Automated Coverslipper (see SOPM "Consul Automated Coverslipper" for instructions).

9.0 Maintenance

All reagents and stains are made fresh before each use.

10.0 Calculations

Not applicable.

11.0 Result Reporting

Not applicable.

12.0 Procedural Notes

Not applicable.

13.0 Limitations

A stain is only as good as the technical considerations and technique used during the staining process. A poor stain may cause difficulty in microscopic evaluation and compromise the cytologic diagnosis.

14.0 Instrumentation Downtime

Not applicable.

15.0 References

Kwik-Diff Stain Kit Package Insert, Thermo Fisher Scientific, Kalamazoo, MI

NON-GYN STAINING

1.0 Principle/Indications

A separate manual staining station is used to stain prepared non-GYN slides with a pap stain. It is important to separately stain GYN from non-GYN (especially fluids) slides in order to prevent cross contamination of cellular material.

2.0 Specimen Requirement/Types

- Non-GYN cytology
  - Urine
  - Rectal
  - Sputum
  - Tzanck smear
  - Breast discharge
  - FNA
    - Various sites, e.g., thyroid, breast, head and neck, prostate, etc.
  - Fluids
    - Various sites, e.g., pleural, peritoneal, synovial, etc.
  - Other miscellaneous

3.0 Supplies/Equipment/Reagents

- Supplies
  - Staining rack
  - Reagent baths and covers
- Equipment
  - Fume hood
- Reagents
  - Gill's Hematoxylin I (PolyScientific), store at room temperature
  - Gill's Hematoxylin II (PolyScientific), store at room temperature
  - OG-6 (PolyScientific), store at room temperature
  - EA-50 (PolyScientific), store at room temperature
  - Bluing Reagent (Thermo), store at room temperature
  - 100% Alcohol, store at room temperature
  - 95% Alcohol, store at room temperature
  - Running water
  - Xylene, store at room temperature

4.0 Instrumentation

Not applicable.

5.0 Calibration

Not applicable.

6.0 Quality Control

- Track lot numbers on all reagents used on designated tracking charts (date opened, lot number, expiration date).
- Documented stain checks are performed each day the stain is performed.

7.0 Environmental Requirements

- Observe universal precautions when handling all specimens. Wear a lab coat, gloves and eye protection.
- All staining is performed under a fume hood (with the exception of the running water steps).

8.0 Operating Procedure

- Fill all reagent baths with appropriate reagents (see diagrams and charts discussed later). For the hematoxylin stain, prepare a 50–50 mixture of Gill's Hematoxylin I and Gill's Hematoxylin II.
- Perform the stain using the non-GYN pap stain protocol discussed later, and proceed to coverslipping on the Consul Automated Coverslipper.

Manual Non-Gyn Pap Stain

Step	Stain/reagent	Time (min)
1	Hematox	1:00
2	Running H20	1:00
3	Bluing Reagent	30 s
4	Running H20	1:30
5	Alcohol 95%	10 dips
6	OG-6	1:30
7	Alcohol 95%	10 dips
8	EA-50	1:00

9	Alcohol 95%	10 dips
10	Alcohol 95%	10 dips
11	Alcohol 95%	10 dips
12	Alcohol 100%	1:00
13	Xylene	1:00
14	Xylene	1:00
15	Xylene	1:00
Approximate Total Time		11:00

Manual NonGyn Pap Stain Flow Chart

← ← ← ← ← ← ← ← ← ← Start

Step	15	14	13	12	11	10	9	8	7	6	5	4	3	2	1
Reagent	Xylene	Xylene	Xylene	Alcohol 100%	Alcohol 95%	Alcohol 95%	Alcohol 95%	EA-50	Alcohol 95%	OG-6	Alcohol 95%	*Running H20	Bluing Reagent	*Running H20	Hematox

*Running H_2O used in sink in Grossing Room

9.0 Maintenance

- All reagents and stains are changed daily and documented on the log sheet "Non-GYN Manual Stain" discussed later.

10.0 Calculations

Not applicable.

11.0 Result Reporting

Not applicable.

12.0 Procedural Notes

- In order to prevent cross contamination, highly cellular specimens processed via direct smear, as well as anal-rectal specimens processed via ThinPrep are stained secondly after all other fluid-type non-GYN specimens prepared via ThinPrep.

- All non-GYN specimens are stained manually on the non-GYN manual staining station and separately from GYN specimens.
- Cover reagents and stains when not in use.
- Non-GYN slides that are received air-dried are stained using the Kwik-Diff procedure).

13.0 Limitations

- Air-dried specimens do not stain well with the Pap stain.
- A stain is only as good as the technical considerations and technique used during the staining process. A poor stain may cause difficulty in microscopic evaluation and compromise the cytologic diagnosis.

14.0 Instrumentation Downtime

Not applicable.

15.0 References

Not applicable.

GRAM STAIN METHOD: HUCKER'S MODIFICATION

1.0 Principle/Indications

- The type of bacterial cell wall directly affects how the Gram stain will react in color. This differential stain divides the majority of bacteria into two groups (Gram-positive and Gram-negative bacteria). The cells are stained with Crystal Violet, and treated with iodine to form a Crystal Violet/iodine complex within the cell. The cell is washed with acetone and then stained again with a Neutral Red counterstain. In the Gram-positive bacteria, the purple Crystal Violet/iodine complex is retained within the cell after washing with acetone. In the Gram-negative bacteria, the Crystal Violet/iodine complex is leached from the cell and they become colorless. The colorless cells then absorb the Neutral Red counterstain.
- The stain will demonstrate the presence of bacteria in a variety of specimen types (Fig. 4.6).

2.0 Specimen Requirement/Types

Biopsy: Paraffin embedded tissue is required, cut at approximately 6 μm.

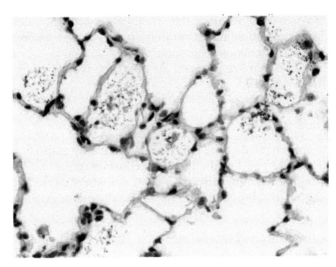

FIGURE 4.6 Hucker-Twort stain is a rapid and simple procedure that stains Gram-positive and Gram-negative bacteria without the use of picric acid. The Fast Green secondary counterstain provides the green background for clear detection of any red Gram-negative bacteria present.

3.0 Supplies/Equipment/Reagents

- Supplies
  - Microscope slides with sections cut at approximately 4–5 μm
  - Staining dishes
  - Slide racks
  - Coverslips
- Equipment
  - Thermo econotherm oven
- Reagents
  - Hucker's Crystal Violet (Poly Scientific), store at room temperature
  - Lugol's Iodine Working Solution (Poly Scientific), store at room temperature
  - Neutral Red 1% Aqueous (Poly Scientific), store at room temperature
  - Gill's II hematoxylin (Thermo), store at room temperature
  - Acetone (Poly Scientific), store at room temperature
  - Distilled water
  - 100% alcohol, store at room temperature
  - 95% alcohol, store at room temperature
  - Xylene, store at room temperature
  - Mounting media, store at room temperature (Fig. 4.7).

STAINS:
   Hucker's stain
   Gram's Iodine
   Safranin O

SAMPLES:
fresh yogurt in 10 mL beaker
1 mL fresh *E. coli* in 13 x 100 mm test tube with **Pasteur pipet**

DEMONSTRATION: Prepare and stain three smears on the same slide (don't cross contaminate):

Position on slide	Specimen in the smear	Reaction to Gram stain
smear 1:	thin smear of fresh yogurt	only Gm+
smear 2:	thin smear of yogurt and a drop of *E. coli* culture	both Gm + and Gm–
smear 3:	thin smear of a drop of *E. coli* culture	only Gm–

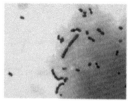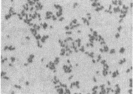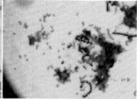

FIGURE 4.7   Both Gram-positive (Gm$^+$) and Gram-negative (Gm$^-$) organisms form a complex of Crystal Violet and iodine within the bacterial cell during the Gram-staining procedure. But Gm$^+$ organisms resist decolorization by alcohol or acetone because, it is thought, dehydration by these solvents markedly decreases cell wall permeability. This dehydration entraps the dye complex within the cell, and Gm + bacteria retain the purple during decolorization while Gm$^-$ do not. In contrast, cell wall permeability of Gm! organisms is increased by ethyl alcohol washing which removes its unusual lipopolysaccharides. This allows the removal of the Crystal Violet–iodine complex from within the cell. The decolorized Gm! cell can then be rendered visible with a suitable counterstain, in this case Safranin O which stains them pink. Pink which adheres to the Gm + bacteria is masked by the purple of the Crystal Violet.

4.0 Instrumentation

Not applicable.

5.0 Calibration

Not applicable.

6.0 Quality Control

Control slides from commercial vendors containing Gram-positive and Gram-negative bacteria are used. See SOPM "Quality Control of Special Stains" for further instructions.

7.0 Environmental Requirements

- Observe universal precautions when handling all specimens. Wear a lab coat, gloves, and eye protection.
- A hood is required when xylene is in use, and when coverslipping slides with mounting media.

8.0 Operating Procedure

- Deparaffinize sections and hydrate slides to water.
- Wash slides in distilled water, 15 dips.
- Stain slides in Hucker's Crystal Violet for 1−2 minutes.
- Wash slides in tap water, 10 dips.
- Place slides in Lugol's Iodine Working Solution for 30 seconds to 1 minute.
- Wash slides in tap water, 10 dips.
- Place slides in acetone for 10−15 dips.
- Wash slides in running tap water for 5−10 minutes.
- Counterstain slides with Neutral Red 1% Aqueous for 30 seconds to 1 minute.
- Wash slides in two changes of tap water, 15 dips each.
- Dehydrate slides by placing in 95% alcohol, 100% alcohol, and xylene for 1 minute each, in that order.
- Coverslip slides with mounting media.

9.0 Maintenance

- Check and document the temperature of the oven with daily use.
- Special stain clearing set-up is changed weekly.

10.0 Calculations

Not applicable.

11.0 Result Reporting

- Reference range: Negative

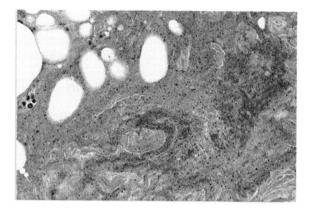

FIGURE 4.8   Examples of Gram-negative rods in two tissue sections.

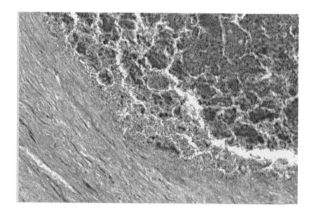

FIGURE 4.9   Turnaround time: 2–3 days.

- Interpretation
  - Gram-positive organisms will appear blue-black
  - Gram-negative organisms will appear red
  - The background will appear pink
- Example: Gram-positive cocci in tissue section (Figs. 4.8 and 4.9)

12.0 Procedural Notes

Not applicable.

13.0 Limitations

- Improperly fixed specimens, specimens exposed to hot paraffin for extended periods of time, and/or specimens inadequately deparaffinized may result in poor staining.
- Alternations in the established stain protocol may affect staining.

14.0 Instrumentation Downtime

Not applicable.

15.0 References

Poly Scientific R&D Corp. Gram Stain Method: Hucker's Modification package insert.

GOMORI'S TRICHROME STAIN

1.0 Principle/Indications

- The trichrome stain involves the application of a red dye in dilute acetic acid to overstain all components in a tissue section. A polyacid is then applied to remove the red dye from collagen and some other components by displacement. A second acid dye (blue or green) in dilute acetic acid is applied which, in turn, displaces the polyacid, resulting in collagen stained in a contrasting color to the initial dye used.
- The stain will demonstrate the presence collagen in the mucosal subepithelial collagen layer of colon tissue. The thickness of the collagen layer will be assessed to confirm microscopic colitis, including lymphocytic colitis and collagenous colitis (Fig. 4.10).

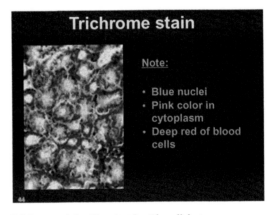

FIGURE 4.10   Trichrome stain: How to identify cell features.

2.0 Specimen Requirement/Types

Colon biopsies will be the primary specimen types. Paraffin embedded tissue is required, cut at approximately 6 μm.

3.0 Supplies/Equipment/Reagents

- Supplies
  - Microscope slides with sections cut at approximately 4−5 μm
  - Staining dishes
  - Slide racks
  - Coverslips
- Equipment
  - Thermo econotherm oven
- Reagents
  - Bouin's fixative (Poly Scientific), store at room temperature
  - Weigert's Iron Hematoxylin Solutions A&B (Poly Scientific), store at room temperature
  - Gomori's One Step Trichrome with Light Green (Poly Scientific), store at room temperature
  - Acetic Acid 0.5% Aqueous (Poly Scientific), store at room temperature
  - Glacial acetic acid (Fisher), store at room temperature
  - Distilled water
  - 95% alcohol, store at room temperature
  - 100% alcohol, store at room temperature
  - Xylene, store at room temperature
  - Mounting media, store at room temperature

4.0 Instrumentation

Not applicable.

5.0 Calibration

Not applicable.

6.0 Quality Control

Sections containing colon tissue showing positive staining for collagen (pathologist confirmed) are used as control slides.

7.0 Environmental Requirements

- Observe universal precautions when handling all specimens. Wear a lab coat, gloves, and eye protection.
- A hood is required when xylene is in use, and when coverslipping slides with mounting media.

8.0 Operating Procedure

- Deparaffinize sections and hydrate slides to water.
- Place in Bouin's fixative in oven at 56°C for 1 hour.
- Wash well in running water or until yellow disappears.
- Stain nuclei with Weigert's iron hematoxylin solutions for 10 minutes.
- Wash well in water.
- Place in Gomori's Trichrome stain for 15–20 minutes.
- Place in Acetic Acid 0.5% for 2 minutes. If sections are too dark, differentiate in Glacial Acetic Acid and rinse in distilled or deionized water.
- Dehydrate slides by placing in 95% alcohol, 100% alcohol, and xylene for 1 minute each, in that order.
- Coverslip slides with mounting media.

9.0 Maintenance

- Check and document the temperature of the oven with daily use. Special stain clearing set-up is changed weekly.

10.0 Calculations

Not applicable.

11.0 Result Reporting

- Reference range: negative
- Interpretation
  - Collagen will appear blue (Figs. 4.11 and 4.12)

12.0 Procedural Notes

Not applicable.

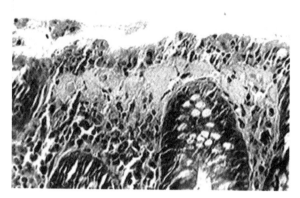

FIGURE 4.11   Example: Colon tissue showing collagen staining.

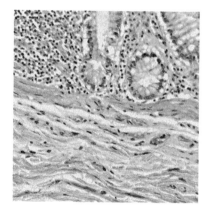

FIGURE 4.12   Human colon tissue stained with Gomori's Trichrome Stain Kit (no collagen).

13.0 Limitations

- Improperly fixed specimens, specimens exposed to hot paraffin for extended periods of time, and/or specimens inadequately deparaffinized may result in poor staining.
- Alternations in the established stain protocol may affect staining.

14.0 Instrumentation Downtime

Not applicable.

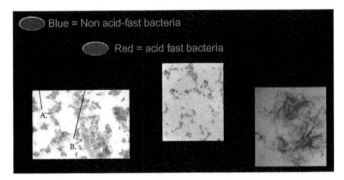

FIGURE 4.13　Example of acid-fast staining in tuberculosis.

15.0 References

- Poly Scientific R&D Corp. Gomori's Trichrome Stain package insert.
- http://esynopsis.uchc.edu/eAtlas/GI/989b.htm

ACID-FAST BACILLI STAIN FOR MYCOBACTERIA

1.0 Principle/Indications

- Mycobacterium species, particularly mycobacterium tuberculosis, are important bacteria to identify due to their ability to cause tuberculosis. Carbol Fuchsin is first applied in the acid-fast method, which stains every cell. After destaining with acid alcohol, only nonacid-fast bacteria destain since they don't have the thick, waxy lipid covering as acid-fast bacteria do. When counterstain is applied (methylene blue), nonacid-fast bacteria pick it up and stain blue. Acid-fast bacteria retain the Carbol Fuchsin and appear red.
- The stain will demonstrate the presence of acid-fast bacteria in a variety of specimen types (Fig. 4.13).

2.0 Specimen Requirement/Types

Biopsy: Paraffin embedded tissue is required, cut at approximately 6 μm.

3.0 Supplies/Equipment/Reagents

- Supplies
  - Microscope slides with sections cut at approximately 4−5 μm
  - Staining dishes

- Slide racks
- Coverslips
- Equipment
  - Thermo econotherm oven
- Reagents
  - Ziehl-Neelsen's Carbol Fuchsin (Poly Scientific), store at room temperature
  - 1% Acid Alcohol (Poly Scientific), store at room temperature
  - Methylene Blue Working Solution (Poly Scientific), store at room temperature
  - Distilled water
  - 100% alcohol, store at room temperature
  - 95% alcohol, store at room temperature
  - Xylene, store at room temperature
  - Mounting media, store at room temperature

4.0 Instrumentation

Not applicable.

5.0 Calibration

Not applicable.

6.0 Quality Control

Control slides from commercial vendors containing acid-fast bacteria are used. Both a positive and negative control must be used when performing an acid-fast stain. The negative control slide does not have to be from a commercial vendor, as long as it contains tissue with nonacid-fast organisms (pathologist confirmed). See SOPM "Quality Control of Special Stains" for further instructions.

7.0 Environmental Requirements

- Observe universal precautions when handling all specimens. Wear a lab coat, gloves, and eye protection.
- A hood is required when xylene is in use, and when coverslipping slides with mounting media.

8.0 Operating Procedure

- Deparaffinize sections and hydrate slides to water.

- Place slides in Ziehl-Neelsen's Carbol Fuchsin Solution for 30 minutes.
- Wash slides well in running water.
- Decolorize slides with Acid Alcohol 1% until sections appear pale pink.
- Wash slides thoroughly in running water for 8 minutes.
- Counterstain slides by dipping one slide at a time in Methylene Blue Working Solution. Sections should appear pale blue when complete.
- Wash slides with tap water, then rinse slides in distilled water.
- Dehydrate slides by placing in 95% alcohol, 100% alcohol, and xylene for 1 minute each, in that order.
- Coverslip slides with mounting media.

9.0 Maintenance

- Check and document the temperature of the oven with daily use (see histology SOPM "Cutting of Tissue Blocks," subsection "Thermo Econotherm Oven").
- Special stain clearing set-up is changed weekly (see SOPM "Gemini Automated Stainer for Hematoxylin and Eosin Staining" for instructions).

10.0 Calculations

Not applicable.

11.0 Result Reporting

- Reference range: Negative
- Interpretation
  - Acid-fast bacilli will appear bright red.
  - Erythrocytes will appear yellowish-orange.
  - Other tissue elements will appear pale blue (Fig. 4.14).

12.0 Procedural Notes

Not applicable.

13.0 Limitations

- Improperly fixed specimens, specimens exposed to hot paraffin for extended periods of time, and/or specimens inadequately deparaffinized may result in poor staining.
- Alternations in the established stain protocol may affect staining.

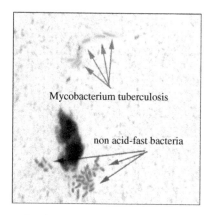

Mycobacterium tuberculosis

non acid-fast bacteria

FIGURE 4.14   An example of acid-fast bacteria in tissue section.

14.0 Instrumentation Downtime

Not applicable.

15.0 References

Poly Scientific R&D Corp. Acid-fast bacilli stain (Ziehl-Neelsen) package insert.

DESTAINING PROCEDURE

1.0 Principle/Indications

Problems or issues in the preparation and staining of cytology slides may require their destaining and restaining as corrective action.

2.0 Specimen Requirement/Types

- GYN cytology
- Non-GYN cytology

3.0 Supplies/Equipment/Reagents

- Supplies
  - Slide racks
  - Staining bath or coplin jar
  - Coverslips
- Equipment: N/A

- Reagents
  - Tap water
  - Xylene, store at room temperature
  - 95% alcohol, store at room temperature
  - 100% alcohol, store at room temperature
  - Hydrochloric acid (Fisher Scientific), store at room temperature
  - Mounting media (mountant) (Consulmount, Thermo), store at room temperature

4.0 Instrumentation

Not applicable.

5.0 Calibration

Not applicable.

6.0 Quality Control

Not applicable.

7.0 Environmental Requirements

Observe universal precautions when handling all specimens. Wear a lab coat, gloves, and eye protection.

8.0 Operating Procedure

- Remove coverslips from slides by soaking them in xylene for 6–8 hours. This assures that all of the mounting media is "cleared" away.
- Place rack of slides in 100% alcohol for 20 minutes, then in 95% alcohol for an additional 15 minutes.
- Place rack of slides in the sink, in a staining bath, and run tap water into the bath for 10 minutes.
- Add 5 mL of hydrochloric acid to staining dish containing 95% alcohol. Dip rack of slides "rapidly" up and down 10 times.
- Rinse in tap water for 1 minute and proceed to 95% alcohol to begin restaining procedure. Follow the routine steps and equipment for whichever individual stain is being performed, with the exception of SurePath slides (see Procedural Notes discussed later).
- Re-coverslip the slides manually or with the Consul Automated.

9.0 Maintenance

Not applicable.

10.0 Calculations

Not applicable.

11.0 Result Reporting

Not applicable.

12.0 Procedural Notes

For SurePath specimens, slides cannot be restained on the PrepStain instrument. Use the Gemini Automated Stainer to restain SurePath slides.

13.0 Limitations

Not applicable.

14.0 Instrumentation Downtime

Not applicable.

15.0 References

Not applicable.

Mechanisms of Disease

Understanding the molecular and cellular mechanisms of disease is one of the key goals of modern biomedical research. It is critical to dissecting the initiation, progression, and dissemination of human diseases, and is vital for the identification of appropriate therapeutic targets and the development of effective treatments.

After the Human Genome Project, the scientific era of omics has emerged to revolutionize our way of studying and learning about cancer (Keusch 2006; Nicholson 2006; Finn 2007; Hamacher et al. 2008). The Greek suffix "ome" means collection or body, the term omics represents the rigorous study of various collections of molecules, biological processes, physiologic functions and structures as systems. It deciphers the dynamic interactions between the numerous components of a biological system to analyze networks, pathways, and interactive relations that exist among them, such as genes, transcripts, proteins, metabolites, and cells (Keusch 2006).

Natural killer (NK) cells are large granular lymphocytes that play a central role in the control of viral infections. NK cells were initially identified through their ability to mediate cellular cytotoxicity against tumor cells.[1] Subsequent studies illustrating activation of NK cells in response to type I interferons (IFNs) also identified them as a component of the innate immune response against pathogens. The contribution of NK cells to the antiviral immune response has been extensively studied in mouse models of viral infections, demonstrating that NK cells not only contain viral replication by killing infected cells during the earliest stages of infection, prior to the development of adaptive immunity, but also play a critical immunoregulatory role during the development of adaptive immunity.[2,3] Although NK cells are considered part of the innate immune system and mediate their effector functions through a number of germ-line-encoded receptors, recent studies have suggested that a subset of NK cells in mice can mediate immunological recall responses to a variety of different haptens and viral pathogens.[4–6] These data indicate that NK cells might comprise a more heterogeneous cell population than initially assumed.

In humans, several rare NK cell deficiencies have been described.[7] Biron et al.[8] first reported a case of a young girl who lacked functional NK cells and experienced a series of viral infections during childhood and adolescence, including infections by multiple herpes viruses. Several subsequent studies have associated human immunodeficiency syndromes that result in complete or partial impairment of NK cell numbers and functions with an increased susceptibility to viral infections, including herpes simplex virus (HSV), varicella zoster virus, cytomegalovirus (CMV), and human papilloma virus, as well as more severe and progressive diseases during childhood[9–11] (Fig. 5.1). These studies established the critical role of functional NK cells in the control of viral infections in humans. Here, we review the mechanisms by which NK cells participate in the control of viral infections, with particular focus on four major human viral infections: CMV (Fig. 5.2), influenza virus (Fig. 5.3B), hepatitis C virus (HCV, Fig. 5.4), and human immunodeficiency virus-1 (HIV-1, Fig. 5.3A). (Figs. 5.5–5.7).

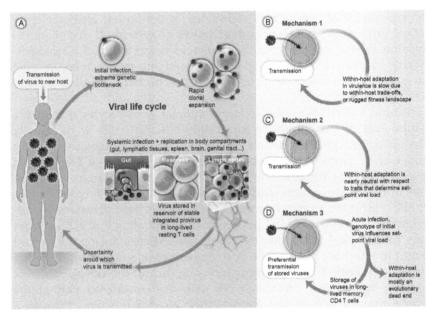

FIGURE 5.1 Virulence and pathogenesis of HIV-1 infection: An evolutionary perspective. Source: *Christophe Fraser, Katrina Lythgoe, Gabriel E. Leventhal, George Shirreff, T. Déirdre Hollingsworth, Samuel Alizon, Sebastian Bonhoeffer, Vol. 343, Issue 6177, 1243727 Science 21 Mar 2014.*

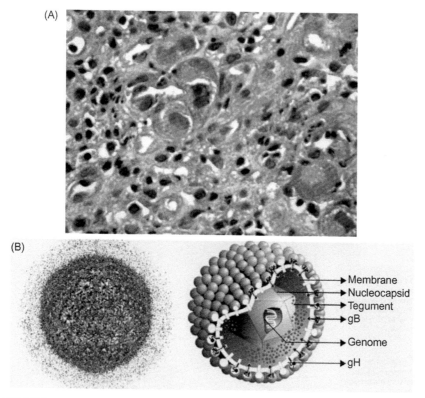

FIGURE 5.2   (A) Cytomegalovirus inclusions in endothelial cells, stained. (B) Hi-resolution schematic diagram of CMV.

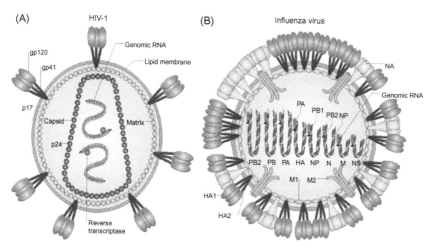

FIGURE 5.3   (A and B) Schematic diagram of HIV-1 and influenza A virus.

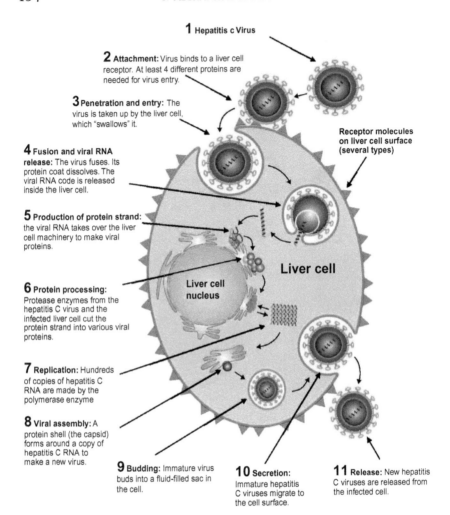

1 Hepatitis c Virus

2 **Attachment:** Virus binds to a liver cell receptor. At least 4 different proteins are needed for virus entry.

3 **Penetration and entry:** The virus is taken up by the liver cell, which "swallows" it.

4 **Fusion and viral RNA release:** The virus fuses. Its protein coat dissolves. The viral RNA code is released inside the liver cell.

5 **Production of protein strand:** the viral RNA takes over the liver cell machinery to make viral proteins.

6 **Protein processing:** Protease enzymes from the hepatitis C virus and the infected liver cell cut the protein strand into various viral proteins.

7 **Replication:** Hundreds of copies of hepatitis C RNA are made by the polymerase enzyme

8 **Viral assembly:** A protein shell (the capsid) forms around a copy of hepatitis C RNA to make a new virus.

9 **Budding:** Immature virus buds into a fluid-filled sac in the cell.

10 **Secretion:** Immature hepatitis C viruses migrate to the cell surface.

11 **Release:** New hepatitis C viruses are released from the infected cell.

Receptor molecules on liver cell surface (several types)

Liver cell

Liver cell nucleus

FIGURE 5.4   Hepatitis C virus life cycle in the human body.

NK cells are generally described as large lymphocytes that lack the expression of the T cell receptor (i.e., CD3 negative), but there is no unifying receptor that identifies all NK cells in different species. NK1.1 can be used to isolate NK cells in some mouse strains, but not all, in which case CD49b (DX5) represents an alternative. Murine NK cells can be further subdivided into four subsets with distinct maturation levels according to their surface expression of CD27 and CD11b.[12] Human NK cells have been classically defined as CD3 − CD56 + lymphocytes, representing about 15% of peripheral blood lymphocytes. CD3 − CD56 + NK cells can be further subdivided into CD56bright NK cells, which lack

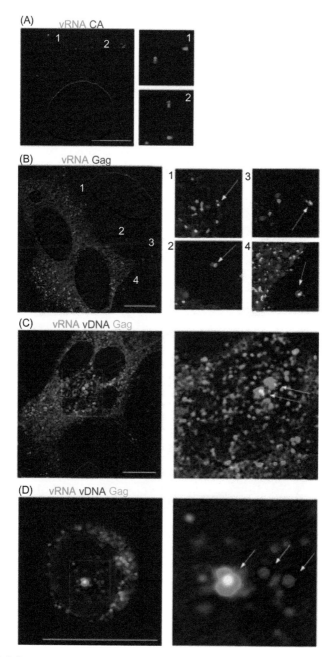

FIGURE 5.5 Multiplex visualization of HIV-1 nucleic acids and protein. (A) Examples of colocalized vRNA and capsid (CA). TZM-bl cells were infected with HIV-1 at an MOI of 0.2; at 2 hpi cells were fixed and stained for unspliced vRNA (PS-1; green), CA (red), and nuclei (blue). Enlarged images indicate colocalization between genomic vRNA of

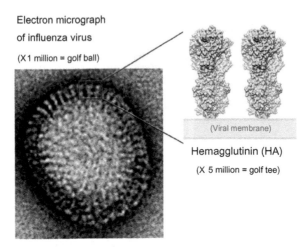

Electron micrograph
of influenza virus
(X1 million = golf ball)

(Viral membrane)

Hemagglutinin (HA)
(X 5 million = golf tee)

FIGURE 5.6 Electron microscopy shows hemagglutinin on the surface of a flu virus particle.

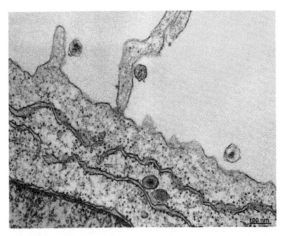

100 nm

FIGURE 5.7 Hepatitis C virus, colored yellow in this transmission electron micrograph, is magnified approximately 100,000.

incoming virus and CA. (B) Apparent formation of nascent virions. TZM-bl cells were infected with HIV-1 at an MOI of 0.2; at 24 hpi cells were fixed and stained for vRNA (PS-1; green), Gag (red), and nuclei (blue). *Arrows* indicate putative virions. (C) Multiplex visualization of transcribed vRNA (PS-2; green) from vDNA (PS-3; red, indicated by white *arrows*) and of translated Gag (gray). TZM-bl cells were infected with HIV-1 at an MOI of 2; at 30 hpi cells were fixed and stained. (D) Discordant expression from nuclear vDNA sites. Jurkat cells were infected with HIV-1 at an MOI of 2; at 24 hpi cells were fixed and stained for vRNA (PS-2; green), vDNA (PS-3; red, indicated with white *arrows*), Gag (gray), and nuclei (blue). *Images were captured with an LSM 880 confocal microscope. Scale bars represent 10 μm.*

the expression of CD16 (Fcγ-receptor) and killer immunoglobulin-like receptor (KIR), and CD56dim NK cells, which express CD16 and KIR.[1,13] In addition, a subset of CD56 − CD16 + NK cells appears to be expanded in chronic viral infections and seems to represent an exhausted/anergic subset of NK cells.[14,15]

NK CELLS IN CMV INFECTION

HCMV is a large double-stranded DNA virus of the subfamily Betaherpesvirinae and is highly prevalent in humans, with 50%−90% of individuals in the United States, and as many as 100% of individuals in developing countries, being seropositive. Infection is usually acquired early in life, and most immunocompetent hosts are asymptomatic. However, CMV can cause severe disease in immunocompromised individuals, such as patients with AIDS or recipients of transplants on immunosuppressive therapy, resulting from the reactivation of latent infection. Furthermore, maternal CMV reactivation or primary infection during pregnancy causes congenital CMV, the most common congenital infection in the developed world, and is associated with long-term sequelae such as hearing loss and developmental delay in about 50% of these infants.[16] HCMV establishes latent persistent infection in monocyte precursors and tissue stroma cells, and persistent immune control is thought to be responsible for the control of the latent infection. HCMV has coevolved with its host for millions of years,[17] resulting in the evolution of a large number of genes that prevent recognition of infected cells by the immune system, including NK cells, and enable the virus to establish persistent infection and dissemination.

NK CELLS IN HIV-1 INFECTION

HIV-1 is a retrovirus that has infected more than 60 million individuals since its initial description in the mid-1980s and has killed more than 30 million individuals. Although all parts of the world are affected by the epidemic, most infected individuals live in sub-Saharan Africa. HIV-1 is transmitted mainly through mucosal routes during sexual exposure by an infected partner, by sharing needles with infected individuals during intravenous drug use, and from mother to child at the time of birth and through breast-feeding. Following acute infection, the virus establishes a chronic infection and a persistent viral reservoir. HIV-1 preferentially infects CD4 + T cells and macrophages and eventually leads to the loss of CD4 + T cells and the development of AIDS in most infected individuals in the absence of antiretroviral therapy. However, the speed of HIV-1 disease progression varies largely between infected individuals, with some individuals developing AIDS within one year of infection, whereas others remain healthy with no manifestations of HIV-1 disease even after more than 25 years of infection.

Overall this book provides an excellent overview of the ongoing molecular revolution that is now transforming pathology and the practice of laboratory medicine. As well as providing a basic reference text for staff in clinical molecular diagnostic laboratories, it also forms a good basis for tutorials and exam preparations. I would highly recommend this book to scientists and health-care professionals working in the field of pathology, including pathology residents, clinicians, and medical students.

References

1. Cooper MA, Fehniger TA, Caligiuri MA. The biology of human natural killer-cell subsets. *Trends Immunol* 2001;**22**:633—40.
2. Altfeld M, Fadda L, Frleta D, Bhardwaj N. DCs and NK cells: critical effectors in the immune response to HIV-1. *Nat Rev Immunol* 2011;**11**:176—86.
3. Vivier E, Tomasello E, Baratin M, Walzer T, Ugolini S. Functions of natural killer cells. *Nat Immunol* 2008;**9**:503—10.
4. O'Leary JG, Goodarzi M, Drayton DL, von Andrian UH. T cell- and B cell-independent adaptive immunity mediated by natural killer cells. *Nat Immunol* 2006;**7**:507—16.
5. Paust S, Gill HS, Wang BZ, Flynn MP, Moseman EA, et al. Critical role for the chemokine receptor CXCR6 in NK cell-mediated antigen-specific memory of haptens and viruses. *Nat Immunol* 2010;**11**:1127—35.
6. Sun JC, Beilke JN, Lanier LL. Adaptive immune features of natural killer cells. *Nature* 2009;**457**:557—61.
7. Orange JS. Human natural killer cell deficiencies and susceptibility to infection. *Microbes Infect* 2002;**4**:1545—58.
8. Biron CA, Byron KS, Sullivan JL. Severe herpesvirus infections in an adolescent without natural killer cells. *N Engl J Med* 1989;**320**:1731—5.
9. de Vries E, Koene HR, Vossen JM, Gratama JW, von dem Borne AE, et al. Identification of an unusual Fcγ receptor IIIa (CD16) on natural killer cells in a patient with recurrent infections. *Blood* 1996;**88**:3022—7.
10. Jawahar S, Moody C, Chan M, Finberg R, Geha R, Chatila T. Natural killer (NK) cell deficiency associated with an epitope-deficient Fc receptor type IIIA (CD16-II). *Clin Exp Immunol* 1996;**103**:408—13.
11. de Haas M, Koene HR, Kleijer M, de Vries E, Simsek S, et al. A triallelic Fcγ receptor type IIIA polymorphism influences the binding of human IgG by NK cell FcγRIIIa. *J Immunol* 1996;**156**:3948—55.
12. Hayakawa Y, Andrews DM, Smyth MJ. Subset analysis of human and mouse mature NK cells. *Methods Mol Biol* 2010;**612**:27—38.
13. Caligiuri MA, Zmuidzinas A, Manley TJ, Levine H, Smith KA, Ritz J. Functional consequences of interleukin 2 receptor expression on resting human lymphocytes. Identification of a novel natural killer cell subset with high affinity receptors. *J Exp Med* 1990;**171**:1509—26.

14. Mavilio D, Benjamin J, Daucher M, Lombardo G, Kottilil S, et al. Natural killer cells in HIV-1 infection: dichotomous effects of viremia on inhibitory and activating receptors and their functional correlates. *Proc Natl Acad Sci USA* 2003;**100**:15011−16.
15. Alter G, Teigen N, Davis BT, Addo MM, Suscovich TJ, et al. Sequential deregulation of NK cell subset distribution and function starting in acute HIV-1 infection. *Blood* 2005;**106**:3366−9.
16. Kenneson A, Cannon MJ. Review and meta-analysis of the epidemiology of congenital cytomegalovirus (CMV) infection. *Rev Med Virol* 2007;**17**:253−76.
17. McGeoch DJ, Dolan A, Ralph AC. Toward a comprehensive phylogeny for mammalian and avian herpesviruses. *J Virol* 2000;**74**:10401−6.

Further Reading

Arnon TI, Markel G, Mandelboim O. Tumor and viral recognition by natural killer cells receptors. *Semin Cancer Biol* 2006;**16**:348−58.

Jost S, Altfeld M. Evasion from NK cell-mediated immune responses by HIV-1. *Microbes Infect* 2012;**14**:904−15.

Arnon TI, Lev M, Katz G, Chernobrov Y, Porgador A, Mandelboim O. Recognition of viral hemagglutinins by NKp44 but not by NKp30. *Eur J Immunol* 2001;**31**:2680−9.

Mandelboim O, Lieberman N, Lev M, Paul L, Arnon TI, et al. Recognition of haemagglutinins on virus-infected cells by NKp46 activates lysis by human NK cells. *Nature* 2001;**409**:1055−60.

Pegram HJ, Andrews DM, Smyth MJ, Darcy PK, Kershaw MH. Activating and inhibitory receptors of natural killer cells. *Immunol Cell Biol* 2011;**89**:216−24.

Bashirova AA, Thomas R, Carrington M. HLA/KIR restraint of HIV: surviving the fittest. *Annu Rev Immunol* 2011;**29**:295−317.

Stewart CA, Laugier-Anfossi F, Vely F, Saulquin X, Riedmuller J, et al. Recognition of peptide- MHC class I complexes by activating killer immunoglobulin-like receptors. *Proc Natl Acad Sci USA* 2005;**102**:13224−9.

Jonsson AH, Yokoyama WM. Natural killer cell tolerance licensing and other mechanisms. *Adv Immunol* 2009;**101**:27−79.

Daniels KA, Devora G, Lai WC, O'Donnell CL, Bennett M, Welsh RM. Murine cytomegalovirus is regulated by a discrete subset of natural killer cells reactive with monoclonal antibody to Ly49H. *J Exp Med* 2001;**194**:29−44.

Dokun AO, Kim S, Smith HR, Kang HS, Chu DT, Yokoyama WM. Specific and nonspecific NK cell activation during virus infection. *Nat Immunol* 2001;**2**:951−6.

Arase H, Mocarski ES, Campbell AE, Hill AB, Lanier LL. Direct recognition of cytomegalovirus by activating and inhibitory NK cell receptors. *Science* 2002;**296**:1323−6.

Bubic I, Wagner M, Krmpotic A, Saulig T, Kim S, et al. Gain of virulence caused by loss of a gene in murine cytomegalovirus. *J Virol* 2004;**78**:7536−44.

Desrosiers MP, Kielczewska A, Loredo-Osti JC, Adam SG, Makrigiannis AP, et al. Epistasis between mouse Klra and major histocompatibility complex class I loci is associated with a new mechanism of natural killer cell-mediated innate resistance to cytomegalovirus infection. *Nat Genet* 2005;**37**:593−9.

Kielczewska A, Pyzik M, Sun T, Krmpotic A, Lodoen MB, et al. Ly49P recognition of cytomegalovirus-infected cells expressing H2-Dk and CMV-encoded m04 correlates with the NK cell antiviral response. *J Exp Med* 2009;**206**:515−23.

Virgin HW, Walker BD. Immunology and the elusive AIDS vaccine. *Nature* 2010;**464**:224−31.

Brainard DM, Seung E, Frahm N, Cariappa A, Bailey CC, et al. Induction of robust cellular and hu- moral virus-specific adaptive immune responses in human immunodeficiency virus-infected humanized BLT mice. *J Virol* 2009;**83**:7305−21.

Dudek TE, No DC, Seung E, Vrbanac VD, Fadda L, et al. Rapid evolution of HIV-1 to functional CD8 + T cell responses in humanized BLT mice. *Sci Transl Med* 2012;**4**:143ra98.

Watkins DI, Burton DR, Kallas EG, Moore JP, Koff WC. Nonhuman primate models and the failure of the Merck HIV-1 vaccine in humans. *Nat Med* 2008;**14**:617–21.

Valentine LE, Watkins DI. Relevance of studying T cell responses in SIV-infected rhesus macaques. *Trends Microbiol* 2008;**16**:605–11.

Hellmann I, Lim SY, Gelman RS, Letvin NL. Association of activating KIR copy number variation of NK cells with containment of SIV replication in rhesus monkeys. *PLoS Pathog* 2011;**7**:e1002436.

Bimber B, O'Connor DH. KIRigami: the case for studying NK cell receptors in SIV + macaques. *Immunol Res* 2008;**40**:235–43.

Colantonio AD, Bimber BN, Neidermyer Jr WJ, Reeves RK, Alter G, et al. KIR polymorphisms modulate peptide-dependent binding to an MHC class I ligand with a Bw6 motif. *PLoS Pathog* 2011;**7**:e1001316.

Rosner C, Kruse PH, Hermes M, Otto N, Walter L. Rhesus macaque inhibitory and activating KIR3D interact with Mamu-A-encoded ligands. *J Immunol* 2011;**186**:2156–63.

Webster RL, Johnson RP. Delineation of multiple subpopulations of natural killer cells in rhesus macaques. *Immunology* 2005;**115**:206–14.

Schmitz JE, Kuroda MJ, Santra S, Sasseville VG, Simon MA, et al. Control of viremia in simian immunodeficiency virus infection by CD8 + lymphocytes. *Science* 1999;**283**:857–60.

Jin X, Bauer DE, Tuttleton SE, Lewin S, Gettie A, et al. Dramatic rise in plasma viremia after CD8 + T cell depletion in simian immunodeficiency virus-infected macaques. *J Exp Med* 1999;**189**:991–8.

Choi EI, Reimann KA, Letvin NL. In vivo natural killer cell depletion during primary simian immunodeficiency virus infection in rhesus monkeys. *J Virol* 2008;**82**:6758–61.

Sun Y, Asmal M, Lane S, Permar SR, Schmidt SD, et al. Antibody-dependent cell-mediated cytotoxicity in simian immunodeficiency virus-infected rhesus monkeys. *J Virol* 2011;**85**:6906–12.

Asmal M, Sun Y, Lane S, Yeh W, Schmidt SD, et al. Antibody-dependent cell-mediated viral inhibition emerges after simian immunodeficiency virus SIVmac251 infection of rhesus monkeys coincident with gp140-binding antibodies and is effective against neutralization-resistant viruses. *J Virol* 2011;**85**:5465–75.

Flores-Villanueva PO, Yunis EJ, Delgado JC, Vittinghoff E, Buchbinder S, et al. Control of HIV-1 viremia and protection from AIDS are associated with HLA-Bw4 homozygosity. *Proc Natl Acad Sci USA* 2001;**98**:5140–5.

Martin MP, Gao X, Lee JH, Nelson GW, Detels R, et al. Epistatic interaction between KIR3DS1 and HLA-B delays the progression to AIDS. *Nat Genet* 2002;**31**:429–34.

Martin MP, Qi Y, Gao X, Yamada E, Martin JN, et al. Innate partnership of HLA-B and KIR3DL1 subtypes against HIV-1. *Nat Genet* 2007;**39**:733–40.

Boulet S, Kleyman M, Kim JY, Kamya P, Sharafi S, et al. A combined genotype of KIR3DL1 high expressing alleles and HLA-B*57 is associated with a reduced risk of HIV infection. *AIDS* 2008;**22**:1487–91.

Boulet S, Sharafi S, Simic N, Bruneau J, Routy JP, et al. Increased proportion of KIR3DS1 homozygotes in HIV-exposed uninfected individuals. *AIDS* 2008;**22**:595–9.

Parsons MS, Boulet S, Song R, Bruneau J, Shoukry NH, et al. Mind the gap: lack of association between KIR3DL1*004/HLA-Bw4-induced natural killer cell function and protection from HIV infection. *J Infect Dis* 2010;**202**(Suppl. 3):S356–60.

Ravet S, Scott-Algara D, Bonnet E, Tran HK, Tran T, et al. Distinctive NK-cell receptor reper-toires sustain high-level constitutive NK-cell activation in HIV-exposed uninfected individuals. *Blood* 2007;**109**:4296–305.

Fellay J, Shianna KV, Ge D, Colombo S, Ledergerber B, et al. A whole-genome association study of major determinants for host control of HIV-1. *Science* 2007;**317**:944−7.

Pereyra F, Jia X, McLaren PJ, Telenti A, de Bakker PI, et al. The major genetic determinants of HIV-1 control affect HLA class I peptide presentation. *Science* 2010;**330**:1551−7.

Kulkarni S, Savan R, Qi Y, Gao X, Yuki Y, et al. Differential microRNA regulation of HLA-C expression and its association with HIV control. *Nature* 2011;**472**:495−8.

Kiepiela P, Leslie AJ, Honeyborne I, Ramduth D, Thobakgale C, et al. Dominant influence of HLA-B in mediating the potential co-evolution of HIV and HLA. *Nature* 2004;**432**:769−75.

Cohen GB, Gandhi RT, Davis DM, Mandelboim O, Chen BK, et al. The selective downregulation of class I major histocompatibility complex proteins by HIV-1 protects HIV-infected cells from NK cells. *Immunity* 1999;**10**:661−71.

Hansasuta P, Dong T, Thananchai H, Weekes M, Willberg C, et al. Recognition of HLA-A3 and HLA-A11 by KIR3DL2 is peptide-specific. *Eur J Immunol* 2004;**34**:1673−9.

Fadda L, O'Connor GM, Kumar S, Piechocka-Trocha A, Gardiner CM, et al. Common HIV-1 peptide variants mediate differential binding of KIR3DL1 to HLA-Bw4 molecules. *J Virol* 2011;**85**:5970−4.

Brackenridge S, Evans EJ, Toebes M, Goonetilleke N, Liu MK, et al. An early HIV mutation within an HLA-B*57-restricted T cell epitope abrogates binding to the killer inhibitory receptor 3DL1. *J Virol* 2011;**85**:5415−22.

Thananchai H, Gillespie G, Martin MP, Bashirova A, Yawata N, et al. Cutting edge: allele-specific and peptide-dependent interactions between KIR3DL1 and HLA-A and HLA-B. *J Immunol* 2007;**178**:33−7.

Thananchai H, Makadzange T, Maenaka K, Kuroki K, Peng Y, et al. Reciprocal recognition of an HLA-Cw4-restricted HIV-1 gp120 epitope by CD8 + T cells and NK cells. *AIDS* 2009;**23**:189−93.

Fadda L, Körner C, Kumar S, van Teijlingen NH, Piechocka-Trocha A, et al. HLA-Cw*0102-restricted HIV-1p24 epitope variants can modulate the binding of the inhibitory KIR2DL2 receptor and primary NK cell function. *PLoS Pathog* 2012;**8**:e1002805.

Alter G, Heckerman D, Schneidewind A, Fadda L, Kadie CM, et al. HIV-1 adaptation to NK- cell-mediated immune pressure. *Nature* 2011;**476**:96−100.

Cerboni C, Neri F, Casartelli N, Zingoni A, Cosman D, et al. Human immunodeficiency virus 1 Nef protein downmodulates the ligands of the activating receptor NKG2D and inhibits natural killer cell-mediated cytotoxicity. *J Gen Virol* 2007;**88**:242−50.

Jost S, Altfeld M. Evasion from NK cell-mediated immune responses by HIV-1. *Microbes Infect* 2012;**14**:904−15.

Choo QL, Kuo G, Weiner AJ, Overby LR, Bradley DW, Houghton M. Isolation of a cDNA clone derived from a blood-borne non-A, non-B viral hepatitis genome. *Science* 1989;**244**:359−62.

Lavanchy D. The global burden of hepatitis C. *Liver Int.* 2009;**29**(Suppl. 1):74−81.

Day CL, Lauer GM, Robbins GK, McGovern B, Wurcel AG, et al. Broad specificity of virus- specific CD4 + T-helper-cell responses in resolved hepatitis C virus infection. *J Virol* 2002;**76**:12584−95.

Lauer GM, Ouchi K, Chung RT, Nguyen TN, Day CL, et al. Comprehensive analysis of CD8 + -T-cell responses against hepatitis C virus reveals multiple unpredicted specificities. *J Virol* 2002;**76**:6104−13.

Grakoui A, Shoukry NH, Woollard DJ, Han JH, Hanson HL, et al. HCV persistence and immune evasion in the absence of memory T cell help. *Science* 2003;**302**:659−62.

Ulsenheimer A, Gerlach JT, Gruener NH, Jung MC, Schirren CA, et al. Detection of functionally altered hepatitis C virus-specific CD4 T cells in acute and chronic hepatitis C. *Hepatology* 2003;**37**:1189−98.

Welsch C, Jesudian A, Zeuzem S, Jacobson I. New direct-acting antiviral agents for the treatment of hepatitis C virus infection and perspectives. *Gut* 2012;**61**(Suppl. 1):i36—46.

Guidotti LG, Chisari FV. Immunobiology and pathogenesis of viral hepatitis. *Annu Rev Pathol Mech Dis.* 2006;**1**:23—61.

Marcello T, Grakoui A, Barba-Spaeth G, Machlin ES, Kotenko SV, et al. Interferons α and λ inhibit hepatitis C virus replication with distinct signal transduction and gene regulation kinetics. *Gastroenterology* 2006;**131**:1887—98.

Grebely J, Petoumenos K, Hellard M, Matthews GV, Suppiah V, et al. Potential role for interleukin-28B genotype in treatment decision-making in recent hepatitis C virus infection. *Hepatology* 2010;**52**:1216—24.

Tillmann HL, Thompson AJ, Patel K, Wiese M, Tenckhoff H, et al. A polymorphism near IL28B is associated with spontaneous clearance of acute hepatitis C virus and jaundice. *Gastroenterology* 2010;**139**:1586—92.

Thomas DL, Thio CL, Martin MP, Qi Y, Ge D, et al. Genetic variation in IL28B and spontaneous clearance of hepatitis C virus. *Nature* 2009;**461**:798—801.

Rauch A, Kutalik Z, Descombes P, Cai T, Di Iulio J, et al. Genetic variation in IL28B is associ- ated with chronic hepatitis C and treatment failure: a genome-wide association study. *Gastroenterology* 2010;**138**:1338—45.

Doherty DG, O'Farrelly C. Innate and adaptive lymphoid cells in the human liver. *Immunol Rev* 2000;**174**:5—20.

Lassen MG, Lukens JR, Dolina JS, Brown MG, Hahn YS. Intrahepatic IL-10 maintains NKG2A + Ly49 − liver NK cells in a functionally hyporesponsive state. *J Immunol* 2010;**184**:2693—701.

Shi FD, Ljunggren HG, La Cava A, Van Kaer L. Organ-specific features of natural killer cells. *Nat Rev Immunol* 2011;**11**:658—71.

Khakoo SI, Thio CL, Martin MP, Brooks CR, Gao X, et al. HLA and NK cell inhibitory receptor genes in resolving hepatitis C virus infection. *Science* 2004;**305**:872—4.

Knapp S, Warshow U, Hegazy D, Brackenbury L, Guha IN, et al. Consistent beneficial effects of killer cell immunoglobulin-like receptor 2DL3 and group 1 human leukocyte antigen-C following exposure to hepatitis C virus. *Hepatology* 2010;**51**:1168—75.

Romero V, Azocar J, Zuniga J, Clavijo OP, Terreros D, et al. Interaction of NK inhibitory receptor genes with HLA-C and MHC class II alleles in hepatitis C virus infection outcome. *Mol Immunol* 2008;**45**:2429—36.

Vidal-Castineira JR, Lopez-Vazquez A, Diaz-Pena R, Alonso-Arias R, Martinez-Borra J, et al. Effect of killer immunoglobulin-like receptors in the response to combined treatment in patients with chronic hepatitis C virus infection. *J Virol* 2010;**84**:475—81.

Marangon AV, Silva GF, de Moraes CF, Grotto RM, Pardini MI, et al. KIR genes and their human leukocyte antigen ligands in the progression to cirrhosis in patients with chronic hepatitis C. *Hum Immunol* 2011;**72**:1074—8.

Alter G, Jost S, Rihn S, Reyor L, Nolan B, et al. Reduced frequencies of NKp30 + NKp46 + , CD161 + , and NKG2D + NK cells in acute HCV infection may predict viral clearance. *J Hepatol* 2010;**55**:278—88.

Yawata M, Yawata N, Draghi M, Partheniou F, Little AM, Parham P. MHC class I-specific inhibitory receptors and their ligands structure diverse human NK-cell repertoires toward a balance of missing self-response. *Blood* 2008;**112**:2369—80.

Rauch A, Laird R, McKinnon E, Telenti A, Furrer H, et al. Influence of inhibitory killer immunoglobulin-like receptors and their HLA-C ligands on resolving hepatitis C virus infection. *Tissue Antigens* 2007;**69**(Suppl. 1):237—40.

Amadei B, Urbani S, Cazaly A, Fisicaro P, Zerbini A, et al. Activation of natural killer cells during acute infection with hepatitis C virus. *Gastroenterology* 2010;**138**:1536—45.

Moesta AK, Norman PJ, Yawata M, Yawata N, Gleimer M, Parham P. Synergistic polymorphism at two positions distal to the ligand-binding site makes KIR2DL2 a stronger receptor for HLA-C than KIR2DL3. *J Immunol* 2008;**180**:3969—79.

Fadda L, Borhis G, Ahmed P, Cheent K, Pageon SV, et al. Peptide antagonism as a mechanism for NK cell activation. *Proc Natl Acad Sci USA* 2010;**107**:10160−5.

Paladino N, Flores AC, Marcos CY, Fainboim H, Theiler G, et al. Increased frequencies of activating natural killer receptors are associated with liver injury in individuals who do not eliminate hepatitis C virus. *Tissue Antigens* 2007;**69**(Suppl. 1):109−11.

Lopez-Vazquez A, Rodrigo L, Martinez-Borra J, Perez R, Rodriguez M, et al. Protective effect of the HLA-Bw4I80 epitope and the killer cell immunoglobulin-like receptor 3DS1 gene against the development of hepatocellular carcinoma in patients with hepatitis C virus infection. *J Infect Dis* 2005;**192**:162−5.

Zuniga J, Romero V, Azocar J, Terreros D, Vargas-Rojas MI, et al. Protective KIR-HLA interac- tions for HCV infection in intravenous drug users. *Mol Immunol* 2009;**46**:2723−77.

Katz G, Gazit R, Arnon TI, Gonen-Gross T, Tarcic G, et al. MHC class I-independent recognition of NK-activating receptor KIR2DS4. *J Immunol* 2004;**173**:1819−25.

Carneiro VL, Lemaire DC, Bendicho MT, Souza SL, Cavalcante LN, et al. Natural killer cell receptor and HLA-C gene polymorphisms among patients with hepatitis C: a comparison between sustained virological responders and non-responders. *Liver Int* 2010;**30**:567−73.

Beziat V, Dalgard O, Asselah T, Halfon P, Bedossa P, et al. CMV drives clonal expansion of NKG2C + NK cells expressing self-specific KIRs in chronic hepatitis patients. *Eur J Immunol* 2012;**42**:447−57.

Bukh J. Animal models for the study of hepatitis C virus infection and related liver disease. *Gastroenterology* 2012;**142**:1279−87.

Wang SH, Huang CX, Ye L, Wang X, Song L, et al. Natural killer cells suppress full cycle HCV infection of human hepatocytes. *J Viral Hepat* 2008;**15**:855−64.

Tseng CT, Klimpel GR. Binding of the hepatitis C virus envelope protein E2 to CD81 inhibits natural killer cell functions. *J Exp Med* 2002;**195**:43−9.

Crotta S, Brazzoli M, Piccioli D, Valiante NM, Wack A. Hepatitis C virions subvert natural killer cell activation to generate a cytokine environment permissive for infection. *J Hepatol* 2010;**52**:183−90.

Crotta S, Stilla A, Wack A, D'Andrea A, Nuti S, et al. Inhibition of natural killer cells through engagement of CD81 by the major hepatitis C virus envelope protein. *J Exp Med* 2002;**195**:35−41.

Yoon JC, Shiina M, Ahlenstiel G, Rehermann B. Natural killer cell function is intact after direct exposure to infectious hepatitis C virions. *Hepatology* 2009;**49**:12−21.

Herzer K, Falk CS, Encke J, Eichhorst ST, Ulsenheimer A, et al. Upregulation of major histo- compatibility complex class I on liver cells by hepatitis C virus core protein via p53 and TAP1 impairs natural killer cell cytotoxicity. *J Virol* 2003;**77**:8299−309.

Nattermann J, Nischalke HD, Hofmeister V, Ahlenstiel G, Zimmermann H, et al. The HLA-A2 restricted T cell epitope HCV core 35-44 stabilizes HLA-E expression and inhibits cytolysis mediated by natural killer cells. *Am J Pathol* 2005;**166**:443−53.

Wen C, He X, Ma H, Hou N, Wei C, et al. Hepatitis C virus infection downregulates the ligands of the activating receptor NKG2D. *Cell Mol Immunol* 2008;**5**:475−8.

Mondelli MU, Varchetta S, Oliviero B. Natural killer cells in viral hepatitis: facts and controversies. *Eur J Clin Investig* 2010;**40**:851−63.

Pár G, Rukavina D, Podack ER, Horányi M, Szekeres-Barthó J, et al. Decrease in CD3-negative- CD8dim + and Vδ2/Vγ9 TcR + peripheral blood lymphocyte counts, low perforin expression and the impairment of natural killer cell activity is associated with chronic hepatitis C virus infection. *J Hepatol* 2002;**37**:514−22.

Bonavita MS, Franco A, Paroli M, Santilio I, Benvenuto R, et al. Normalization of depressed natural killer activity after interferon-α therapy is associated with a low frequency of relapse in patients with chronic hepatitis C. *Int J Tissue React* 1993;**15**:11−16.

Corado J, Toro F, Rivera H, Bianco NE, Deibis L, De Sanctis JB. Impairment of natural killer (NK) cytotoxic activity in hepatitis C virus (HCV) infection. *Clin Exp Immunol* 1997;**109**:451−7.

Morishima C, Paschal DM, Wang CC, Yoshihara CS, Wood BL, et al. Decreased NK cell fre- quency in chronic hepatitis C does not affect ex vivo cytolytic killing. *Hepatology* 2006;**43**:573−80.

Ahlenstiel G, Titerence RH, Koh C, Edlich B, Feld JJ, et al. Natural killer cells are polarized toward cytotoxicity in chronic hepatitis C in an interferon-alfa-dependent manner. *Gastroenterology* 2010;**138**:325−35.

De Maria A, Fogli M, Mazza S, Basso M, Picciotto A, et al. Increased natural cytotoxicity receptor expression and relevant IL-10 production in NK cells from chronically infected viremic HCV patients. *Eur J Immunol* 2007;**37**:445−55.

Oliviero B, Varchetta S, Paudice E, Michelone G, Zaramella M, et al. Natural killer cell functional dichotomy in chronic hepatitis B and chronic hepatitis C virus infections. *Gastroenterology* 2009;**137**:1151−60.

Duesberg U, Schneiders AM, Flieger D, Inchauspe G, Sauerbruch T, Spengler U. Natural cyto- toxicity and antibody-dependent cellular cytotoxicity (ADCC) is not impaired in patients suffering from chronic hepatitis C. *J Hepatol* 2001;**35**:650−7.

Golden-Mason L, Madrigal-Estebas L, McGrath E, Conroy MJ, Ryan EJ, et al. Altered natural killer cell subset distributions in resolved and persistent hepatitis C virus infection following single source exposure. *Gut* 2008;**57**:1121−8.

Guidotti LG, Chisari FV. Noncytolytic control of viral infections by the innate and adaptive immune response. *Annu Rev Immunol* 2001;**19**:65−91.

Pelletier S, Drouin C, Bedard N, Khakoo SI, Bruneau J, Shoukry NH. Increased degranulation of natural killer cells during acute HCV correlates with the magnitude of virus-specific T cell responses. *J Hepatol* 2010;**53**:805−16.

Cheent K, Khakoo SI. Natural killer cells and hepatitis C: action and reaction. *Gut* 2011;**60**:268−78.

Bonorino P, Ramzan M, Camous X, Dufeu-Duchesne T, Thelu MA, et al. Fine characterization of intrahepatic NK cells expressing natural killer receptors in chronic hepatitis B and C. *J Hepatol* 2009;**51**:458−67.

Harrison RJ, Ettorre A, Little AM, Khakoo SI. Association of NKG2A with treatment for chronic hepatitis C virus infection. *Clin Exp Immunol* 2010;**161**:306−14.

Jinushi M, Takehara T, Tatsumi T, Kanto T, Miyagi T, et al. Negative regulation of NK cell activities by inhibitory receptor CD94/NKG2A leads to altered NK cell-induced modulation of dendritic cell functions in chronic hepatitis C virus infection. *J Immunol* 2004;**173**:6072−81.

Golden-Mason L, Kelly AM, Doherty DG, Traynor O, McEntee G, et al. Hepatic interleukin 15 (IL-15) expression: implications for local NK/NKT cell homeostasis and development. *Clin Exp Immunol* 2004;**138**:94−101.

Nattermann J, Feldmann G, Ahlenstiel G, Langhans B, Sauerbruch T, Spengler U. Surface ex- pression and cytolytic function of natural killer cell receptors is altered in chronic hepatitis C. *Gut* 2006;**55**:869−77.

Gunturi A, Berg RE, Forman J. The role of CD94/NKG2 in innate and adaptive immunity. *Immunol Res* 2004;**30**:29−34.

Kramer B, Körner C, Kebschull M, Glässner A, Eisenhardt M, et al. Natural killer p46High expression defines a natural killer cell subset that is potentially involved in control of hepatitis C virus replication and modulation of liver fibrosis. *Hepatology* 2012;**56**:1201−13.

Golden-Mason L, Cox AL, Randall JA, Cheng L, Rosen HR. Increased natural killer cell cyto- toxicity and NKp30 expression protects against hepatitis C virus infection in high-risk individuals and inhibits replication in vitro. *Hepatology* 2010;**52**:1581−9.

Morens DM, Taubenberger JK. Pandemic influenza: certain uncertainties. *Rev Med Virol* 2011;**21**:262−84.

World Health Organization. 2009. Influenza (seasonal). Factsheet No. 211, April, World Health Org., Geneva. http://www.who.int/mediacentre/factsheets/fs211/en/.

Thompson WW, Shay DK, Weintraub E, Brammer L, Bridges CB, et al. Influenza-associated hospitalizations in the United States. *JAMA* 2004;**292**:1333−40.

Thompson WW, Shay DK, Weintraub E, Brammer L, Cox N, et al. Mortality associated with influenza and respiratory syncytial virus in the United States. *JAMA* 2003;**289**:179−86.

Thompson WW, Weintraub E, Dhankhar P, Cheng PY, Brammer L, et al. Estimates of US influenza-associated deaths made using four different methods. *Influenza Other Respir Viruses* 2009;**3**:37−49.

Doherty PC, Topham DJ, Tripp RA, Cardin RD, Brooks JW, Stevenson PG. Effector CD4 + and CD8 + T-cell mechanisms in the control of respiratory virus infections. *Immunol Rev* 1997;**159**:105−17.

Thomas PG, Keating R, Hulse-Post DJ, Doherty PC. Cell-mediated protection in influenza infection. *Emerg Infect Dis* 2006;**12**:48−54.

Ennis FA, Meager A, Beare AS, Qi YH, Riley D, et al. Interferon induction and increased natural killer-cell activity in influenza infections in man. *Lancet* 1981;**2**:891−3.

Gregoire C, Chasson L, Luci C, Tomasello E, Geissmann F, et al. The trafficking of natural killer cells. *Immunol Rev* 2007;**220**:169−82.

Reynolds CW, Timonen T, Herberman RB. Natural killer (NK) cell activity in the rat. I. Isolation and characterization of the effector cells. *J Immunol* 1981;**127**:282−7.

Stein-Streilein J, Bennett M, Mann D, Kumar V. Natural killer cells in mouse lung: surface phenotype, target preference, and response to local influenza virus infection. *J Immunol* 1983;**131**:2699−704.

Nogusa S, Ritz BW, Kassim SH, Jennings SR, Gardner EM. Characterization of age-related changes in natural killer cells during primary influenza infection in mice. *Mech Ageing Dev* 2008;**129**:223−30.

Stein-Streilein J, Guffee J. In vivo treatment of mice and hamsters with antibodies to asialo GM1 increases morbidity and mortality to pulmonary influenza infection. *J Immunol* 1986;**136**:1435−41.

Stein-Streilein J, Guffee J, Fan W. Locally and systemically derived natural killer cells participate in defense against intranasally inoculated influenza virus. *Reg Immunol* 1988;**1**:100−5.

Liu B, Mori I, Hossain MJ, Dong L, Takeda K, Kimura Y. Interleukin-18 improves the early defence system against influenza virus infection by augmenting natural killer cell-mediated cytotoxicity. *J Gen Virol* 2004;**85**:423−8.

Dong L, Mori I, Hossain MJ, Kimura Y. The senescence-accelerated mouse shows aging-related defects in cellular but not humoral immunity against influenza virus infection. *J Infect Dis* 2000;**182**:391−6.

Abdul-Careem MF, Mian MF, Yue G, Gillgrass A, Chenoweth MJ, et al. Critical role of natural killer cells in lung immunopathology during influenza infection in mice. *J Infect Dis* 2012;**206**:167−77.

Verbist KC, Rose DL, Cole CJ, Field MB, Klonowski KD. IL-15 participates in the respiratory innate immune response to influenza virus infection. *PLoS One* 2012;**7**:e37539.

Gazit R, Gruda R, Elboim M, Arnon TI, Katz G, et al. Lethal influenza infection in the absence of the natural killer cell receptor gene Ncr1. *Nat Immunol* 2006;**7**:517−23.

Glasner A, Zurunic A, Meningher T, Lenac Rovis T, Tsukerman P, et al. Elucidating the mech- anisms of influenza virus recognition by Ncr1. *PLoS One* 2012;**7**:e36837.

Achdout H, Meningher T, Hirsh S, Glasner A, Bar-On Y, et al. Killing of avian and swine influenza virus by natural killer cells. *J Virol* 2010;**84**:3993−4001.

Narni-Mancinelli E, Jaeger BN, Bernat C, Fenis A, Kung S, et al. Tuning of natural killer cell reactivity by NKp46 and Helios calibrates T cell responses. *Science* 2012;**335**:344—8.

Hashimoto G, Wright PF, Karzon DT. Antibody-dependent cell-mediated cytotoxicity against influenza virus-infected cells. *J Infect Dis* 1983;**148**:785—94.

Jegerlehner A, Schmitz N, Storni T, Bachmann MF. Influenza A vaccine based on the extracellular domain of M2: weak protection mediated via antibody-dependent NK cell activity. *J Immunol* 2004;**172**:5598—605.

Ahlenstiel G, Martin MP, Gao X, Carrington M, Rehermann B. Distinct KIR/HLA compound genotypes affect the kinetics of human antiviral natural killer cell responses. *J Clin Investig* 2008;**118**:1017—26.

La D, Czarnecki C, El-Gabalawy H, Kumar A, Meyers AF, et al. Enrichment of variations in KIR3DL1/S1 and KIR2DL2/L3 among H1N1/09 ICU patients: an exploratory study. *PLoS One* 2011;**6**:e29200.

Aranda-Romo S, Garcia-Sepulveda CA, Comas-Garcia A, Lovato-Salas F, Salgado-Bustamante M, et al. Killer-cell immunoglobulin-like receptors (KIR) in severe A (H1N1) 2009 influenza infections. *Immunogenetics* 2012;**64**:653—62.

Arnon TI, Achdout H, Lieberman N, Gazit R, Gonen-Gross T, et al. The mechanisms controlling the recognition of tumor- and virus-infected cells by NKp46. *Blood* 2004;**103**:664—72.

Draghi M, Pashine A, Sanjanwala B, Gendzekhadze K, Cantoni C, et al. NKp46 and NKG2D recognition of infected dendritic cells is necessary for NK cell activation in the human response to influenza infection. *J Immunol* 2007;**178**:2688—98.

Du N, Zhou J, Lin X, Zhang Y, Yang X, et al. Differential activation of NK cells by influenza A pseudotype H5N1 and 1918 and 2009 pandemic H1N1 viruses. *J Virol* 2010;**84**:7822—31.

Jost S, Reardon J, Peterson E, Poole D, Bosch R, et al. Expansion of 2B4+ NK cells and decrease in NKp46+ NK cells in response to influenza. *Immunology* 2010;**132**:516—26.

Owen RE, Yamada E, Thompson CI, Phillipson LJ, Thompson C, et al. Alterations in receptor binding properties of recent human influenza H3N2 viruses are associated with reduced natural killer cell lysis of infected cells. *J Virol* 2007;**81**:11170—8.

Zhang M, Gaschen B, Blay W, Foley B, Haigwood N, et al. Tracking global patterns of N-linked glycosylation site variation in highly variable viral glycoproteins: HIV, SIV, and HCV envelopes and influenza hemagglutinin. *Glycobiology* 2004;**14**:1229—46.

Achdout H, Arnon TI, Markel G, Gonen-Gross T, Katz G, et al. Enhanced recognition of human NK receptors after influenza virus infection. *J Immunol* 2003;**171**:915—23.

Achdout H, Manaster I, Mandelboim O. Influenza virus infection augments NK cell inhibition through reorganization of major histocompatibility complex class I proteins. *J Virol* 2008;**82**:8030—7.

He XS, Holmes TH, Zhang C, Mahmood K, Kemble GW, et al. Cellular immune responses in children and adults receiving inactivated or live attenuated influenza vaccines. *J Virol* 2006;**80**:11756—66.

Long BR, Michaelsson J, Loo CP, Ballan WM, Vu BA, et al. Elevated frequency of gamma interferon-producing NK cells in healthy adults vaccinated against influenza virus. *Clin Vaccine Immunol* 2008;**15**:120—30.

Denney L, Aitken C, Li CK, Wilson-Davies E, Kok WL, et al. Reduction of natural killer but not effector CD8 T lymphocytes in three consecutive cases of severe/lethal H1N1/09 influenza A virus infection. *PLoS One* 2010;**5**:e10675.

Heltzer ML, Coffin SE, Maurer K, Bagashev A, Zhang Z, et al. Immune dysregulation in severe influenza. *J Leukoc Biol* 2009;**85**:1036—43.

Jost S, Quillay H, Reardon J, Peterson E, Simmons RP, et al. Changes in cytokine levels and NK cell activation associated with influenza. *PLoS One* 2011;**6**:e25060.

Guo X, Chen Y, Li X, Kong H, Yang S, et al. Dynamic variations in the peripheral blood lymphocyte subgroups of patients with 2009 pandemic H1N1 swine-origin influenza A virus infection. *Virol J* 2011;**8**:215.

Fox A, Le NM, Horby P, van Doorn HR, Nguyen VT, et al. Severe pandemic H1N1 2009 infection is associated with transient NK and T deficiency and aberrant CD8 responses. *PLoS One* 2012;**7**:e31535.

Guo H, Kumar P, Moran TM, Garcia-Sastre A, Zhou Y, Malarkannan S. The functional impair- ment of natural killer cells during influenza virus infection. *Immunol Cell Biol* 2009;**87**:579−89.

Mao H, Tu W, Qin G, Law HK, Sia SF, et al. Influenza virus directly infects human natural killer cells and induces cell apoptosis. *J Virol* 2009;**83**:9215−22.

Altfeld Marcus, Fadda Lena, Frleta Davor, Bhardwaj Nina. DCs and NK cells: critical effectors in the immune response to HIV-1. *Nature Reviews Immunology* 2011;**11**:176−86.

Index

Note: Page numbers followed by "*f*" and "*t*" refer to figures and tables, respectively.

A

aCGH. *See* Array–comparative genome
  hybridization (Array–CGH)
Acid-fast
  bacteria, 144, 144*f*, 147*f*
  method, 144
Acid-fast bacilli stain for mycobacteria
  calculations, 146
  calibration, 145
  environmental requirements, 145
  instrumentation, 145
    downtime, 147
  limitations, 146
  maintenance, 146
  operating procedure, 145–146
  principle/indications, 144
  procedural notes, 146
  quality control, 145
  references, 147
  result reporting, 146
  specimen requirement/types, 144
  supplies/equipment/reagents, 144–145
Adenine, 55, 56*f*
Alleles, 55, 66–67
  gene, 65, 68
  risk-increasing, 64–65, 70–71
  of SNP, 65–66
Amended Reports, 29–31
Anal-rectal ThinPrep specimens, 91
Anatomic pathology monitors, 28
Anticipation, 67
Apoptosis, 158
Array–comparative genome hybridization
  (Array–CGH), 61–62
ASCUS/SIL ratio assessment, 34
Attributable risk, 71, 72*t*
Autopsy, 60–61

B

Basal cell carcinoma, 20–21
Biopsy, 27, 78, 135
  bags, 80

  cervical, 84
  reports, 28
  specimen collection,
    104–105
  sponges, 82–83
  surgical, 50–51
Blood, 10*t*, 13
Bloodstream
  dissemination in, 7–10
  infections due to RNA viruses, 9*f*
  pathogenesis of selected virus infections,
    10*t*
  virus spread through, 9*f*
Bondmax, 125
  stainer, 108
  systems, 111–112
BRCA gene, 20
Breast cancer, 20
  lymph node-negative,
    62
  molecular stratification, 63
Breast discharge, 92, 103, 128, 132

C

Cancer
  analyses, 70
  types, 67–68
CAP. *See* College of American Pathologists
  (CAP)
CD56bright NK cells, 154–157
CDC. *See* Centers for Disease Control and
  Prevention (CDC)
CE-marked tests, 24
Cellular
  pathogenesis, 4–5
  susceptibility, 3
  transcriptional factors, 1
Centers for Disease Control and
  Prevention (CDC), 63
Cervical biopsy, 84
Cervical cone/LEEP specimens, 84

Chemotherapy, 20
  decision for inclusion, 63
  personalized, 20
Chip-based testing, 20
Chromosome rearrangements, 69
  detection, 25–26
CLIA. *See* Clinical Laboratory Improvement
    Amendments (CLIA)
Clinical human genetics
  context, 60–72
    cancer analyses, 70
    CNV, 69–70
    deletions and insertions in DNA,
      66–67
    direct-to-consumer GWA testing
      services, 70–71
    functional polymorphisms, 71–72
    mechanisms for disease, 72
    molecular medicine assays in
      pathology, 62–65
    MSI, 67–68
    SNPs, 65–66, 71–72
Clinical human medical genetics
  context, 60–72
  DNA, 55–60
Clinical Laboratory Improvement
    Amendments (CLIA), 63
Clinical utility, 63–65
Clinical validity, 63–65
  genomic test, 64
Clonality assessment, 22
CMV. *See* Cytomegalovirus (CMV)
CNV. *See* Copy number variation (CNV)
COBAS
  BRAF mutation test, 24
"Cobblestone" surface, 98
College of American Pathologists (CAP), 43
  HistoQIP program, 44–45
  non-GYN cytopathology program, 44
  PIP in surgical pathology, 44
Colloid nodules, 91
Comprehensive molecular assays,
    validation of, 26
Congenital anomalies, 14
Congenital infections, 14
Constitutional disease, 13
Copy number variation (CNV), 20, 61–62,
    69–70
CYP2D6. *See* Cytochrome p450 2D6
    (CYP2D6)
Cystic fibrosis, 158
Cytochrome p450 2D6 (CYP2D6), 69

Cytokines, 14–15
Cytologic atypia, 91
  solid nodules with, 91
Cytology
  GYN cytology abnormal case review, 47
  material, 39
  non-GYN cytology case review, 47
  quality control, 45–47
Cytomegalovirus (CMV), 13, 152, 153*f*
Cytopathology monitors, 32–36
Cytosine, 55–56, 56*f*
Cytotechnologist competency, 41–43
Cytotechnologist Dotting Protocol, 47
Cytotechnologist Misses Log, 42
Cytotechnologist screening accuracy,
    assessment of, 35–36

D
Dasatinib, 69
De novo HCV infections, 14–15
Decalcification, 82, 110
Defective T cell immunity, 14–15
Deletions in DNA, 66–67
Deoxyribonucleic acid (DNA), 55–60, 56*f*
  cell-free, 20
  chips, 61–62
  fingerprinting, 158
  of host cells, 13
  human DNA molecule, 71–72
  megasatellite, 57*f*
  microarrays, 61–62
  polymerase, 25
  polymorphisms, 158
  sequence, 57
    mutations, 60
    polymorphisms, 71–72
  strands, 58
  types, 57–58
Deoxyribose, 56, 58
Destaining procedure. *See also* Grossing
    procedures
  calculations, 149
  calibration, 148
  environmental requirements, 148
  instrumentation, 148
    downtime, 149
  limitations, 149
  maintenance, 149
  operating procedure, 148
  principle/indication, 147
  procedural notes, 149
  quality control, 148

references, 149
result reporting, 149
specimen requirement/types, 147
supplies/equipment/reagents, 147–148
Diabetes, 20–22
Diabetic nephropathy, 66–67
Dinucleotide repeats, 67
Direct cell damage, 1, 4
Direct to consumer (DTC), 21
  genomic testing, 21
  GWA testing services, 70–71
Disease(s), 158
  mechanisms for, 72
  NK cells
    in CMV infection, 157
    in HIV-1 infection, 157–158
Dissemination
  in bloodstream, 7–10
  in nerves, 11
DNA. *See* Deoxyribonucleic acid (DNA)
DTC. *See* Direct to consumer (DTC)

E

EGFR. See Epidermal growth factor
    receptor (*EGFR*)
Enhancer sequences, 5
Enteroviruses, 4–5
Epidermal growth factor receptor (*EGFR*),
    20
Epstein-Barr virus, 4–5
Estrogen receptor (ER), 63
Extracellular spread, 5–6
Extradepartmental Consult Agreement,
    31
Extradepartmental consultations, 40

F

FDA. *See* Food and Drug Administration
    (FDA)
Fetus
  Down syndrome in, 20
  implantation in, 5
  infection, 14
Fever, 13
Fine needle aspiration (FNA), 89, 103–104
FISH analysis. *See* Fluorescent in situ
    hybridization analysis (FISH
    analysis)
Fixation principles, 80–81
Fluids, 104, 132
  hazardous, 120
  surface, 6

Fluorescent in situ hybridization analysis
    (FISH analysis), 20, 25–26
FNA. *See* Fine needle aspiration (FNA)
Food and Drug Administration (FDA), 62
  FDA-approved COBAS *BRAF* mutation
    test, 24
Formal competency assessments, 43
Formalin-based decalcification solution, 82
Functional polymorphisms, 71–72
Fusion transcripts, 22

G

Gastroenteritis viruses, 7
Gastrointestinal tract (GI tract), 2, 84
Genetic factors, 65–66
Genital tract, 13
Genome wide association studies (GWAS),
    21–22
Genome-wide SNP screens, 70–71
Genomic(s), 20
  applications, 19–20
  DNA alterations, 23–24
  genomic-profile, 63
  technology, 20
  testing, 20–22
Germline mutations, 70
GI tract. *See* Gastrointestinal tract (GI tract)
Gomori's trichrome stain
  calculations, 142
  calibration, 141
  environmental requirements, 142
  instrumentation, 141
    downtime, 143
  limitations, 143
  maintenance, 142
  operating procedure, 142
  principle/indications, 140
  procedural notes, 142
  quality control, 141
  references, 144–147
  result reporting, 142
    colon tissue showing collagen staining,
      143*f*
    human colon tissue stained, 143*f*
  specimen requirement/types, 141
  supplies/equipment/reagents, 141
Gram stain method, 135–140
  calculations, 138
  calibration, 137
  environmental requirements, 138
  instrumentation, 137
    downtime, 140

Gram stain method (*Continued*)
  limitations, 140
  maintenance, 138
  operating procedure, 138
  principle/indications, 135
  procedural notes, 139
  quality control, 138
  result reporting, 138–139
  specimen requirement/types, 135
  supplies/equipment/reagents, 136
Gram-negative bacteria, 135, 137*f*
Gram-positive bacteria, 135, 137*f*
Grossing Log Sheet, 86
Grossing procedures, 77–88. *See also*
    Destaining procedure
  calculations, 87
  calibration, 78
  environmental requirements, 79
  instrumentation, 78
    downtime, 88
  limitations, 87
  maintenance, 87
  operating procedure, 79–87
  principle/indications, 77–78
  procedural notes, 87
  quality control, 78
  references, 88
  result reporting, 87
  specimen requirement/types, 78
  supplies/equipment/reagents, 78
Guanine, 55, 56*f*
GWA studies, 71
GWAS. *See* Genome wide association
    studies (GWAS)
Gynecological cytology (GYN cytology), 27,
    84, 89–92, 93*f*. *See also* Non-
    gynecological cytology (Non-GYN
    cytology)
  abnormal case review, 47
  cytopathology reports, 89

H
H&E. *See* Hematoxylin and eosin (H&E)
Haplotype
HCMV, 157
HCV. *See* Hepatitis C virus (HCV)
Helicobacter pylori infection, 66–67
Hematoxylin and eosin (H&E), 121
Hematoxylin stain, 133
Hepatitis B virus, 4–5
Hepatitis C virus (HCV), 152, 154*f*, 156*f*
  infection, 14–15

  NK cells in, 14–15
  RNA, 14–15
Hereditary hemochromatosis, 65–66
Herpes simplex virus (HSV), 152
Herpesvirus, 5–6, 13
HFE gene. *See* Human hemochromatosis
    gene (HFE gene)
HIV. *See* Human immunodeficiency virus
    (HIV)
HPV. *See* Human papilloma virus (HPV)
HSV. *See* Herpes simplex virus (HSV)
Hucker-Twort stain, 136*f*
Hucker's modification, 135–140
Human DNA, 66
  molecule, 71–72
  sequence, 55
Human hemochromatosis gene (HFE gene),
    65–66
Human immunodeficiency virus (HIV), 4,
    13
  HIV-1, 152, 157–158
    virulence and pathogenesis, 152*f*
Human NK cells, 154–157
Human papilloma virus (HPV), 152
Human papilloma virus (HPV) in situ
    procedures
  calculations, 121
  calibration, 108
  environmental requirements, 110
  instrumentation, 107
    downtime, 125
  limitations, 124
  maintenance, 120
  operating procedure, 110–120
  principle/indication, 106
  procedural notes, 123
  quality control, 108–110
  references, 125–128
  result reporting, 121–123, 121*f*
  specimen requirement/types, 107
  supplies/equipment/reagents, 107
Human viral infections, 152
167-gene assay, 20
Huntington's disease, 158

I
ICGC. *See* International Cancer Genome
    Consortium (ICGC)
IFN defense mechanisms. *See* Interferon
    defense mechanisms (IFN defense
    mechanisms)
IFNs. *See* Interferons (IFNs)

IHC. *See* Immunohistochemistry (IHC)
IL-1RA gene. *See* Interleukin-1-receptor antagonist gene (IL-1RA gene)
IL28B gene, 14–15
Immunohistochemistry (IHC), 20, 106–127
  calculations, 121
  calibration, 108
  environmental requirements, 110
  instrumentation, 107
    downtime, 125
  limitations, 124
  maintenance, 120
  operating procedure, 110–120
  principle/indication, 106
  procedural notes, 123
  quality control, 108–110
  references, 125–128
  result reporting, 121–123, 121*f*
  specimen requirement/types, 107
  staining, 20
  supplies/equipment/reagents, 107
  techniques, 106
In situ hybridization (ISH), 25–26
In situ testing, 111
In vitro diagnostic medical devices (IVDMD), 62
In vitro diagnostic product (IVD product), 62
Incubation period, 2, 11
Indirect cell damage, 1
Infected migratory cells, 6
Innate immune effector cells, 14–15
Insertion/deletion polymorphisms (indel polymorphisms), 66
Insertions in DNA, 66–67
Interferon defense mechanisms (IFN defense mechanisms), 1
Interferons (IFNs), 151–152
  IFN-γ, 14–15
  IFN-λ, 14–15
Interleukin-1-receptor antagonist gene (IL-1RA gene), 66–67
International Cancer Genome Consortium (ICGC), 62
Intracellular spread, 5–6
Intrauterine device (IUD), 85
IOM. *See* US Institute of Medicine (IOM)
Ion Torrent Personal Genome Machine (IT-PGM), 25
ISH. *See* In situ hybridization (ISH)
IT-PGM. *See* Ion Torrent Personal Genome Machine (IT-PGM)

IUD. *See* Intrauterine device (IUD)
IVD product. *See* In vitro diagnostic product (IVD product)
IVDMD. *See* In vitro diagnostic medical devices (IVDMD)

J
JV papovavirus, 5

K
Killer immunoglobulin-like receptor (KIR), 154–157
KIR. *See* Killer immunoglobulin-like receptor (KIR)
Kwik-Diff staining, 128–132, 128*f*
  calculations, 131
  calibration, 129
  environmental requirements, 130
  instrumentation, 129
    downtime, 131
  limitations, 131
  maintenance, 131
  operating procedure, 130–131
  principle/indications, 128
  procedural notes, 131
  quality control, 130
  result reporting, 131
  specimen requirement/types, 128
  supplies/equipment/reagents, 129

L
Laboratory information system (LIS), 28
  assessment of incorrect entries into, 37
Laboratory-developed tests (LDTs), 62
Large colonic polyps, 84
Last menstrual period (LMP), 102
LDTs. *See* Laboratory-developed tests (LDTs)
LIR-1. *See* Leukocyte immunoglobulin-like receptor 1 (LIR-1)
LIS. *See* Laboratory information system (LIS)
Lithotomy position, 97
Live virus vaccines, 3
LMP. *See* Last menstrual period (LMP)
Localized skin infections, 7
Loss of Heterozygosity (LOH), 68
Low throughput assays, 24–25
Lymph, 13
  lymph node-negative breast cancer, 62
Lynch syndrome-associated tumors, 22

M

Malaise, 13
Manual Non-Gyn pap stain, 133–134
Maraviroc, 70
Markers, 71–72
Maternal viremia, 14
Medical genetics, 55
Megasatellite DNAs, 58
MicroRNA (miRNA), 61–62
Microsatellite instability (MSI), 67–68
  analysis, 22
  types of chromosomal rearrangements,
    68*f*
Microsatellites, 67
  LOH, 68
Milk, 13
Minisatellite DNAs, 58
miRNA. *See* MicroRNA (miRNA)
Molecular applications in pathology, 22–23
Molecular diagnostics, 19–20
Molecular medicine
  in action
    acid-fast bacilli stain for mycobacteria,
      144–147
    destaining procedure, 147–149
    Gomori's trichrome stain, 140–144
    Gram stain method, 135–140
    grossing procedures, 77–88
    immunohistochemistry and HPV in
      situ procedures, 106–127
    Kwik-Diff staining, 128–132, 128*f*
    Non-Gyn staining, 132–135
    specimen adequacy, 89–92
    specimen collection instructions,
      92–106
  assays in pathology, 62–65
Molecular pathology, 1, 20
  congenital infections, 14
  detection of chromosomal
    rearrangements, 25–26
  incubation period, 11
  molecular applications, 22–23
  multiplication in target organs, 12–13
  mutation detection
    low throughput assays, 24–25
  NK cells in HCV infection, 14–15
  pathogenesis, 1–11
  quality management program, 26–52
  shedding of virus, 13
  technological challenges, 23–24
  validation of comprehensive molecular
    assays, 26

Moloney murine leukemia retrovirus, 5
MSI. *See* Microsatellite instability (MSI)
Multiplication in target organs, 12–13
Multitude of molecular tests, 23–24
Mutation detection
  low throughput assays, 24–25
Mycobacteria, acid-fast bacilli stain for,
  144–147
Mycobacterium tuberculosis, 144

N

National Cancer Institute (NCI), 62
Natural killer cells (NK cells), 151–152
  in CMV infection, 157
  in hepatitis C virus infection, 14–15
  in HIV-1 infection, 157–158
NCI. *See* National Cancer Institute (NCI)
Negative predictive validity (NPV), 64
Nerves
  dissemination in, 11
  virus spread through, 12*f*
Neural infection, 2
Next-generation sequencing methods (NGS
  methods), 21, 26
  NGS-based methods, 25
NGS methods. *See* Next-generation
  sequencing methods (NGS methods)
Nitrogenous base, 56
NK cells. *See* Natural killer cells (NK cells)
NKG2A receptor, 15
NKT cells, 14–15
Non-GYN cytology. *See* Non-gynecological
  cytology (Non-GYN cytology)
Non-Gyn staining, 132–135
  calculations, 134
  calibration, 133
  environmental requirements, 133
  instrumentation, 133
  instrumentation downtime, 135
  limitations, 135
  maintenance, 134
  operating procedure, 133–134
  principle/indications, 132
  procedural notes, 134–135
  quality control, 133
  result reporting, 134
  specimen requirement/types, 132
  supplies/equipment/reagents, 132
Non-gynecological cytology (Non-GYN
  cytology), 27, 47, 91. *See also*
  Gynecological cytology (GYN
  cytology)

case review, 47
non-GYN cytopathology reports, 89
non-GYN manual stain, 134
non-GYN reports, 28
NPV. *See* Negative predictive validity (NPV)
Nucleoside, 56
Nucleotide, 56

O

Omics, 151
  omics-based tumor biomarker tests, 62
OncoCarta panels, 24–25
Oncology, 20

P

Pap/HPV HR correlation assessment, 33–34
Paps received with patient identifier, 36
Parallel next-generation methods, 20
Pathogenesis, 1–11
  cellular pathogenesis, 4–5
  dissemination in bloodstream, 7–10
  dissemination in nerves, 11
  local replication and local spread, 5–7
    virus spread during localized infection, 6f
  of selected virus infection, 7t
Pathologist
  competency, 40
  referral rate comparison to actual abnormal rate, 35
Pathologist Consensus Agreement assessment, 30–31
Pathology, 19
  molecular applications in, 22–23
Patient ID (PID), 48
Performance improvement program (PIP), 41
Phosphodiester bonds, 57
Physical barriers, 3
Picornaviruses, 7
PID. *See* Patient ID (PID)
PIP. *See* Performance improvement program (PIP)
Plastic "broom-like" brush, 100
PMA. *See* Premarket Approval (PMA)
PMI. *See* Precision Medicine Initiative (PMI)
POC. *See* Products of conception (POC)
Poliomyelitis, 7–10

Polioviruses, 4–5
Polymorphisms, 65–66
Positive predictive validity (PPV), 64
Positive vimentin staining, 110
PPV. *See* Positive predictive validity (PPV)
Precision medicine, 19–20
Precision Medicine Initiative (PMI), 62
Premarket Approval (PMA), 62
Products of conception (POC), 80, 84
Proficiency testing, 43
Proteins, 55, 58, 59f
Purines, 55
Pyrimidines, 55–56

Q

Quality assessment, 23
"Quality Control Gradings" sheet, 41
Quality control of special stains, 138
"Quality Control Rescreen Record" sheet, 42
Quality indicators, 28, 32–38
Quality management program
  calculations, 52
  calibration, 27
  environmental requirements, 27
  instrumentation, 27
    downtime, 52
  limitations, 52
  maintenance, 52
  operating procedure, 27–51
  principle/indications, 26–27
  procedural notes, 52
  quality control, 27
  references, 52
  result reporting, 52
  specimen requirement/types, 27
  supplies/equipment/reagents, 27

R

Rabies virus, 4–5, 11
Reagent inventory screen, 116–117
Recombination frequency (Rf), 72
Rectal, 102
Repetitive DNA, 57
REporting recommendations for tumor MARKer studies (REMARK studies), 62
Retroviruses, 13
Rf. *See* Recombination frequency (Rf)
Rhinoviruses, 4–5

Ribonucleic acid (RNA), 58
  polymerases, 1, 58–60
  RNA-based sequencing approach, 25–26
  tumor viruses, 13
Ribosomal RNA (rRNA), 60
Ribosome, 66
Ribosomes, 4
RNA. *See* Ribonucleic acid (RNA)
Rotaviruses, 7
Routine biopsy reports, 28
rRNA. *See* Ribosomal RNA (rRNA)

S
Saliva, 13
SBH. *See* Sequencing by hybridization
    (SBH)
Second NGS-based test, 20
Secondary viremia, 7–10
Sequencing by hybridization (SBH), 61–62
Sequencing human genomes, 21
Sequencing-by-synthesis approach, 25
Shedding of virus, 13
Single copy DNA, 57
Single-nucleotide polymorphisms (SNPs),
    20, 61–62, 65–66, 71–72
Skin, 84
"Slide History" screen, 117
Small nuclear RNAs (snRNA), 60
SNPs. *See* Single-nucleotide polymorphisms
    (SNPs)
snRNA. *See* Small nuclear RNAs (snRNA)
Solid nodules
  with cytologic atypia, 91
  with inflammation, 91
Solid surface chips, 61–62
Somatic mutations, 70
SOP. *See* Standard operating procedure
    (SOP)
Specimen, 79
Specimen adequacy
  calculations, 91
  calibration, 89
  environmental requirements, 89
  instrumentation, 89
    downtime, 92
  limitations, 92
  maintenance, 91
  operating procedure, 89–91
  principle/indications, 89
  procedural notes, 92
  quality control, 89

  references, 92
  result reporting, 92
  specimen requirement/types, 89
  supplies/equipment/reagents, 89
Specimen collection instructions
  calculations, 106
  calibration, 95
  environmental requirements, 96
  instrumentation, 95
    downtime, 106
  limitations, 106
  maintenance, 105
  operating procedure, 96–105
  principle/indications, 92
  procedural notes, 106
  quality control, 95
  references, 106
  result reporting, 106
  specimen requirement/types, 92–94, 93f
  supplies/equipment/reagents, 94–95
Speculum, 98
Spinocereballar ataxia (S. ataxia), 67
SpiraBrush, 84
Sputum, 103
  specimens, 91
Staining
  with monoclonal antibody V9 vimentin,
    110
  process, 131, 135
  protocols, 118–119
Standard operating procedure (SOP), 24, 77
Surgical biopsies received without proper
    identification, 38
Surgical pathology monitors, 37–38

T
T-cell receptor gene rearrangements, 22
Targeted therapies, 23
TCGA. *See* The Cancer Genome Atlas
    (TCGA)
Tetranucleotide repeats, 67
The Cancer Genome Atlas (TCGA), 23, 62
ThinPrep Imaging System or FocalPoint GS
    Imaging System, 43
Thymine, 55–56, 56f
Tissues, 80
  staining, 124
TKI. *See* Tyrosine kinase inhibitor (TKI)
Tracking charts, 130
Transcriptome analysis, 20–21
Trastuzumab, 23

Trichrome stain, 140, 140*f*
Trinucleotide, 67
  repeats, 67
Tropism, 2
Tumor heterogeneity, 26
Tumor viruses, 13
Turnaround time assessment, 29–31
Two-Step Miss Log, 42
Type III IFN, 14–15
Tyrosine kinase inhibitor (TKI), 20, 69
Tzanck smear, 103

U
Unsatisfactory rate, 32
Urine, 102
US Institute of Medicine (IOM), 62

V
Validation process, 26
Varicella zoster virus, 152

Viral/virus(es), 4–5, 7–10
  affinity, 2
  antigens, 11, 13
  infections, 2–3, 11
  progeny, 7–10
  replication, 12–13
  shedding of, 13
  spread, 5–6
    during localized infection, 6*f*
  tissue tropism, 4–5
  tropism, 5
Viremic infection, 2
Virions, 2–3
Virulence characteristics, 3

W
Whole-genome sequencing,
  20, 20–21
WindoPath LIS, 46

Printed and bound by CPI Group (UK) Ltd, Croydon, CR0 4YY

03/10/2024

01040420-0019